Practical FLOWER ARRANGING

Jean Taylor

PHOTOGRAPHY BY DOUGLAS RENDELL

LINE DRAWINGS BY RON HAYWARD

HAMLYN

London · New York · Sydney · Toronto

ACKNOWLEDGEMENTS

The Author would like to thank Michael Minifie
for his assistance with the photography and
Mr and Mrs K. Berisford for giving her facilities
to photograph some of the arrangements in their
home.

Additional photographs of plants were provided by
Pat Brindley, Ernest Crowson and Harry Smith.

First published in 1974 by
The Hamlyn Publishing Group Limited
London · New York · Sydney · Toronto
Astronaut House, Feltham, Middlesex, England

Second impression, 1974

Filmset in Great Britain by
Filmtype Services Limited, Scarborough

Printed by Litografia A. Romero, S.A.
Tenerife (Spain)

Contents

Introduction

More and more men and women of all ages are learning how to arrange flowers and it has become a very popular creative activity. This is probably because there is great satisfaction in working with beautiful, natural materials in a way that requires no special talent and which need not be time-consuming or expensive. Flowers, leaves and other types of plant material are easily available and there are many varieties from which to choose.

Apart from the enjoyment of actually arranging the flowers there are other related interests; plants can be grown in the garden or home especially for use in flower arrangements; the search for containers, accessories and new materials leads to exciting excursions to city and countryside; containers can be constructed and adapted at home without any advanced techniques; the study of the long history of flower arrangement is fascinating; an appreciation of the other arts grows with an increased knowledge of design.

New friends can be made through sharing a common interest and in flower arrangement this can be extended in the happy atmosphere of clubs and classes, both of which now exist all over the British Isles, the United States of America and in many other parts of the world.

Many people learn the art so that they can enhance their homes with beautiful and colourful flowers. Others enjoy the challenge and stimulation provided by entering competitive flower arrangement shows and some enjoy the exploration of plant material as the medium of a different form of art.

Whatever the reason, enthusiasm is quick to grow as knowledge increases but it is essential to understand the practical details before the art can be truly explored. These are not difficult and simply concern such things as the type of equipment used; the preparation of flowers and leaves to last for a long time in water; methods of holding stems in position. There are also certain easily understood guides for arranging flowers based on universal ideas about design.

Once these have been assimilated there is a fascinating and lifelong interest to enjoy using the lovely materials provided by Nature.

Equipment

The basic equipment for flower arrangement is not expensive or elaborate but, as with all arts and crafts, it is a necessity. Further equipment can be bought at a later stage if needed. Tools and other items are not hard to come by and are available for sale at florists, ironmongers, garden centres and flower arrangement clubs.

BASIC EQUIPMENT

Many designs can be made with the following:

Flower scissors	Wire netting, ½ yd. of
Knife	1-in. mesh
Buckets	Reel of florists' wire
Watering-can	Elastic bands
Polythene sheet	Sand
Two containers	Stub wire
Two food tins	Cocktail sticks
Plastic foam blocks	Dowel or skewer
Plastic foam pinholder	Several bases
Plastic foam saucer	Cover-ups
One 3-in. pinholder	A well-type pinholder
Plasticine	
Wire netting, 1 yd. of	
2-in. mesh	

FURTHER EQUIPMENT

More containers and	Secateurs
bases	Flower cutters
Pinholders of other	Candlecups
sizes	Accessories
Tubes	

Tools for Cutting

Domestic scissors are not good cutters for stems and special flower scissors are available which cut all but thick, woody stems and also the thin wire that is sometimes used in flower arrangement. In the early stages of learning to arrange flowers these scissors are all that are necessary.

There are more expensive flower cutters that are a delight to use and a good investment for the more advanced flower arranger. They cut all stems with the exception of really thick, woody branches for which secateurs are needed. They also cut any wire used by flower arrangers.

Secateurs may be in your tool-box already, as they are used in the garden for pruning. They are occasionally useful for cutting heavy branches for flower arrangement.

A sharp knife cuts stems very cleanly and may be used in place of scissors but may also cause cut fingers. It is needed for scraping stems.

Buckets, Watering-can, Polythene

One or two tall buckets will be necessary for soaking stems in water. There is one sold in two sizes, which is made especially for flowers. It has two handles for lifting, one on either side, in place of the normal central handle that may damage flower heads.

A small watering-can, with a long thin spout, is

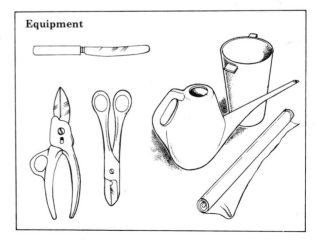

Equipment

A group of useful containers. Below the white figurine are two well-type pinholders. A candlecup has been fixed to the candlestick.

necessary for filling containers with water and for 'topping-up'.

A sheet of heavy polythene is useful for collecting the rubbish, which is inevitable. This makes clearing up quicker and easier.

Containers

This is the term used for receptacles which contain the stem ends of flowers. They may or may not hold water. Formerly they were called vases, a term that is rarely used now. Many people think that elaborate and expensive containers are a necessity but this is not so since flower arrangements can look equally beautiful in simple, inexpensive containers. A good buy to begin with is a baking dish in a dull colour and about 12 inches long. It is versatile for arrangements and can also be used (well cleaned) for cooking. Another good buy is a bowl shape with a stem which lifts the flowers up attractively and allows plant material to flow down at the sides. Tins cost nothing and are useful, but the surfaces should be covered with something such as paint or Fablon, or the tins should be concealed in some way, as they are not attractive enough in them-

selves to be shown. Other containers can be collected as you progress and discover your needs. Small ones are not easy to use and should be avoided at first.

SUPPORTS FOR FLOWERS

Flowers can be dropped into a container and left alone – but they will not look as attractive as when they are arranged in such a way that every flower is clearly seen. This means positioning the flowers carefully, and in order to do this, supports are necessary for the stems. It is well worth the slight effort to use these supports because less flowers are needed when they are well displayed and the arrangement is then economical as well as attractive.

The supports most often used are:
1. Plastic foam, sold under several trade names, which absorbs and retains water.
2. Pinholders, which are lead bases containing sharp vertical pins.
3. Wire netting.
4. A combination of all or any two of the above.

6

Plastic Foam

This is the easiest support to use as stems are held exactly in position, but as it cannot be used indefinitely it is more expensive than the others. It is sold in blocks which are very light until filled with water, when they become extremely heavy. A block measuring 9 in. by 4½ in. by 3 in. weighs 2 oz. before wetting and 4 lb. when it has taken up water, so it can hold more than 3 pints of water. Plastic foam can hold more stems than a pinholder.

Stem ends. These are simply pushed into the foam in any position, enabling a variety of designs to be made. The only unsuitable stems are soft ones, which give way as you push them in, and very large branches which are so heavy that the soft foam collapses under their weight. It is wise not to keep putting stems in and then taking them out again because a hole is made each time and eventually there are so many holes that there is no support for the stems. Decide where each stem should go, push it in and then leave it if possible.

Preparation of the foam. The foam is sold in blocks which can be cut wet or dry, with a knife, to fit the container.

Drop the block into cold water, deeper than itself, and without pushing it down leave it to take up water gradually. This will cause it to sink and when it has sunk level with the surface of the water, it has taken in all the water it can hold. No more water is absorbed by longer soaking. A round, 3 in. in diameter and 2½ in. deep, will take about 10 minutes and a block of the size mentioned previously will take about 20 minutes. There are 'instant' foams on the market which absorb water more quickly – if you buy these follow the manufacturers' instructions.

When the foam has absorbed water, place it in the container. If some of it stands above the rim of the container stems may be inserted at an angle allowing the design to flow down at the sides. This cannot be accomplished as easily with a pinholder or wire netting.

Keeping the foam in place. The foam may be so firmly wedged in the container that no extra support is needed, but in some containers it may slip about, especially if it is standing well above the rim.

The foam can be held more firmly in position by several methods:

1. It may be used with a pinholder made especially for this purpose with pins set wide apart so that the foam is pressed on to the pins. If a normal pinholder is used it becomes clogged up.

2. Special plastic saucers can be bought inexpensively which hold the foam securely with

Blocks of plastic foam soaking. The round on the left is fully soaked and level with the water

A special pinholder made to hold plastic foam in position. The pins are set wider apart than the usual kind

Left: A plastic saucer which holds the foam securely by means of a built-in circle
Right: Stems can flow downwards if the foam stands above the container

Foam can be placed in a polythene bag

A 3-in. pinholder showing an impaled stem

prongs or a small built-in plastic circle. These saucers are useful for low table arrangements and for taking flowers already arranged (to the nurses' delight) to hospital.

3. With wire netting as described on page 10.

Aftercare. The surface of the foam soon dries out in a warm room and a little water should be poured on to it every day, after the flowers have been arranged. To save leakage on to the furniture when doing this, it is better to cut the foam a little smaller than the container so that any extra water slips down the sides and is held in the container. The foam can be used several times, depending upon the amount of plant material that has been placed in it, and until it contains too many holes with no support for stems. In between use, keep it in a polythene bag because once it has completely dried out it cannot absorb water again.

Containers which do not hold water. A great advantage of plastic foam is that it can be used in a container which is not intended to hold water, such as a wooden box without a waterproof lining. The foam should be placed into a polythene bag which is tied tightly, the spare polythene being cut off. Place the bagged foam into the container and then push the stems through the polythene and into the foam. Woody stems pierce the polythene more easily than soft ones, but a hole can be made with a skewer and then the soft stems can be inserted. It is better not to make holes in the bottom of the polythene bag or water may leak out.

Pinholders

These are also called needlepoint holders, kenzans or frogs. They are lead bases in which sharp vertical pins are embedded. The best buy is a heavy one with long pins placed close together. It may seem expensive but will be worth the money in the long run. Shapes and sizes vary but the most useful to start with is a round shape of 3 in. diameter.

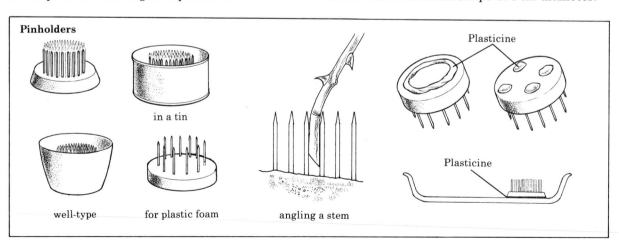

Pinholders

in a tin

well-type · for plastic foam · angling a stem

Plasticine

Plasticine

Pinholders are especially successful in shallow containers, with designs using little plant material. Small pinholders are not heavy enough, are difficult to use, and are a waste of money at the beginning.

Stem ends. Stems are pushed straight down on to the pins and can either be impaled on them or slipped between them. The stems may then be angled by applying gentle pressure. Slender stems cannot be held firmly and are not suitable but they can still be used with a pinholder if placed into a section of a hollow stem which is itself impaled on the pins. Beware of damaging fingers on the sharp pins when using a pinholder.

Preparation of the pinholder. Simply place the pinholder in the container in any position. The weight of the lead should keep it in place. Make sure that the container is deep enough for water to stand above the top of the pins.

Keeping pinholders in place. Sometimes a pinholder slips about. This can be prevented by anchoring it with Plasticine, sealing strip or similar compounds sold for this purpose. *The container, Plasticine and pinholder must be quite dry.* Form the Plasticine into a sausage, or three or four blobs, and press on to the underside of the pinholder. Press the pinholder firmly down on to the bottom of the container and give a small twist. It should then be quite firm and the container could be turned upside down without dislodging the pinholder.

Well-type pinholder. This is the term used for a pinholder incorporated into a small heavy metal dish which holds water. A satisfactory one can be made by placing a pinholder into a deep food tin from which the lid has been removed. The tin should be painted with dark matt paint to prevent the shine of metal being seen through the flowers. As well-type pinholders are not meant to be seen, they should be concealed with 'cover-ups' of plant material, stones, glass and so on. This type of

One-inch-mesh wire netting bent into a U-shape

container is very versatile since it can be used in place of a more expensive container, on a variety of bases, and is therefore a good buy for a beginner. As it holds only a small quantity of water, very little plant material should be used in it. The water soon evaporates and well-type pinholders should be topped up daily when in use.

Aftercare. After using any pinholder, wash and dry it before storing. The Plasticine may be left on, providing it is dry before it is used again. A wire brush can be used to clean away any bits of plant material lodged in the pinholder.

Wire Netting

This is available by the yard and can be cut with flower scissors. The selvedge is stiff and should be removed. Plastic-coated netting is bulky to use. The 2-in. mesh is suitable for crumpling into deep containers and 1-in. mesh may be used as an extra support over plastic foam or a pinholder.

Stem ends. These are placed into the gaps formed

Left: 1-in. mesh wire netting in a deep urn with a pinholder for impaling stem ends. *Middle:* Rubber bands holding wire netting in place in a bowl. *Right:* Wire netting held down with reel wire in a well-type pinholder

9

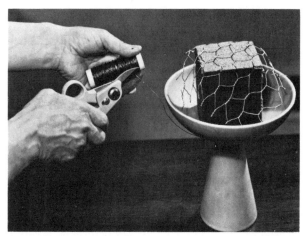

One-inch-mesh wire netting used as a cap over foam

when the 2-in. netting is crumpled. The placement of stems is not so accurate as with plastic foam or a pinholder, but it is an inexpensive support and useful for very big, deep containers and large arrangements.

Preparation of the wire netting. For a large deep container, cut a piece of mesh as wide as the cavity and about three times its depth. Bend it into a 'U' shape with the cut ends upwards and then crumple it down into the container so that the cavity is filled, but not so crowded that stems cannot be inserted. The cut ends should be left standing above the rim of the container as they can be used for winding around heavy stems to provide a second support.

Keeping the netting in place. The wire netting often wobbles about unless it is held in place firmly. This can be done by several methods:
1. A pinholder can be placed on the bottom of the

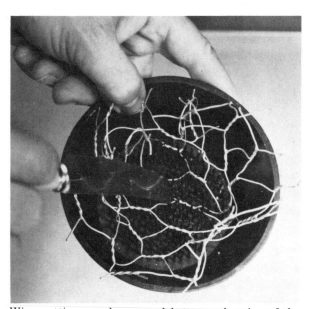

Wire netting can be pressed between the pins of the pinholder with a knife

container below the netting. The first stem, placed through the netting and impaled on to the pinholder, will hold it down.
2. The netting can be held firmly in a low bowl by placing a heavy rubber band (or more than one) over both container and netting. Alternatively, lengths of string or wire from a reel may be tied around them both.
3. A length of reel wire can be attached to one side of the netting, passed around the bottom of the container or its stem, and then attached to the netting on the other side. More than one length may be used in this way for extra firmness. If the container has handles, the wire can be attached to these and the netting.

Netting combined with plastic foam. A very reliable support is formed when a cap of un-crumpled 1-in. wire netting is placed over the top of plastic foam; 2-in. mesh should not be used as it cuts into the soft foam. Cut a piece of netting which fits the top of the foam and is big enough to be bent over the sides. Keep it as flat as possible and attach it with reel wire (as 3 above) for a very firm support.

Netting combined with a pinholder. The 2-in.-mesh netting can be crumpled into a ball with the cut ends upwards and pressed down on to a pinholder in a shallow container. Some of the wire can be pushed between the pins with a knife or scissors. The first stem impaled on the pinholder holds the netting in place. This is useful for heavy stems which need extra support.

Sand

Supporting flowers in a tall narrow container can be a problem. A pinholder on the bottom means that only very long-stemmed flowers can be used and wire netting can become a rusty muddle without giving accurate support. A successful method is to fill the container to within two inches of the top with wet sand. Some stems can be held in place with this alone, but still better support is supplied if a pinholder is placed on top of the sand. It does not sink down and you can work higher up and with shorter stems. The container can be filled with water to give two inches of clear water on top of the sand. Plastic foam may also be used rested on the top of the sand.

Cocktail Sticks and Dowel

Fruit is an interesting material for arrangement but it can roll about if not secured and wire can spoil it if it is needed later for eating. To make fruit stay in place, a cocktail stick can be pressed halfway into a piece of fruit and the other half pressed into another piece. Little damage is done. However, when placing fruit into plastic foam or a pinholder, a cocktail stick is seldom strong enough and a piece of dowel or a wooden meat skewer is necessary. One end is pushed into the fruit and the other into the foam or pinholder. Grapes may be held in place by wiring the stem (through the grapes) to a piece of dowel or a skewer.

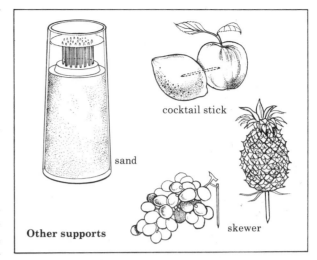

cocktail stick

sand

Other supports

skewer

Stub Wires

These are short strong wires in various lengths and gauges, the higher the gauge the finer the wire. Most flowers appear more natural if they are not wired but occasionally flower heads are heavy and need extra support or a bent stem may need a splint. Leaves, especially those which have been preserved or dried, may need wire to replace their stems.

Heavy flower heads. Run a strong wire into the stem guiding it with the other hand until it is near the flower. Cut the wire to allow one inch to extend beyond the stem end. When the stem is placed into plastic foam the wire goes in first and gives extra support. Make sure the stem end reaches water. This is useful for hyacinth. Camellias often drop off their stems and can be wired by placing two wires through the calyx at right angles. Bend the wires back to form a stem.

Floppy stems. Some stems, such as those of tulips, can be very floppy. Pierce the stem near the flower head with a wire. Push it through the stem and bend down a small amount. Twist the remainder down the stem in big twists and place stem and wire together into the plastic foam.

Bent stems. Guide a wire into the stem until it reaches beyond the bent part. Cut the wire off level with the stem end.

Pine cones. Two stub wires are needed for each cone. Place them into the lower scales on either side of the cone and parallel to each other. Twist them together on either side, bend them down below the cone and then twist them around each other. The cone now has a false stem. Several cones may be clustered together and used as a group in a design, the wires being placed into the foam or pinholder.

Nuts. Drill a hole in the bottom and glue in a wire.

Leaves. These may be wired in one of the following ways:

1. Push a wire through a leaf about half an inch above the place where the stem and leaf join. Bend the wire gently so that the two ends point downwards and are parallel. Wind one end of the wire around the other, catching in any leaf stem.

2. Place a stub wire along the back of a leaf and almost reaching the tip. Stick a length of Sellotape over it and on to the leaf to hold the wire in position.

3. Make a stitch with fine wire across the leaf. Turn back the wire on the underside and twist the ends together around any remaining stem.

Mechanics

This is the collective term used by flower arrangers for all equipment which holds plant material in position. It is well worthwhile practising mechanics, as good supports are essential for successful arrangements. There is nothing more frustrating than a wobbly flower arrangement and it takes twice as long to complete if the mechanics are not firm in the first place. It is also quite a disaster to have an arrangement fall over in the

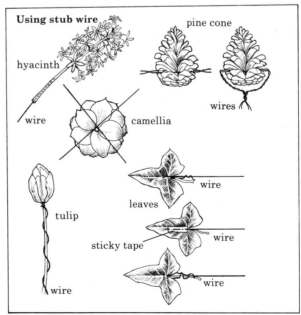

Using stub wire

pine cone

hyacinth

wire

camellia

wires

leaves

wire

tulip

sticky tape

wire

wire

wire

11

The grouping of plant material shown on the opposite page dropped in position in a narrow-necked container

middle of a church service or a dinner party and very embarrassing for the arranger. It is tempting to spend only a little time on the mechanics because one is longing to get on with arranging the flowers, but time spent on making quite certain the supports are firm is always worthwhile. For a purer effect when the arrangement is complete, it is better to keep mechanics simple. If they are elaborate the result is often a flower arrangement which is contrived in appearance.

OTHER EQUIPMENT

Cover-ups for Mechanics

Mechanics are not attractive and need to be hidden. Often the container itself does this, especially if it is a deep one. If plastic foam shows above the container it is soon hidden by cutting the stems of a few leaves very short and placing them close to the plastic foam and quite flat. The same applies to wire netting. A pinholder and a food tin or well-type pinholder can also be covered with plant material but sometimes this can spoil the clarity of a design and some other material looks better. Small pieces of driftwood and coral are useful for concealment and also add something interesting to the design.

A collection of compatible objects can be made for this purpose. Stones, bark and wood are always attractive for natural looking designs, shattered windscreen glass looks lovely over pinholders in glass containers, shells and coral can add interesting textures.

Suggestions:

stones	coral	bark
pebbles	shells	glass chunks
gravel	driftwood	windscreen glass

Candlecup

This is a device which can turn a candlestick or a narrow-necked bottle into a container. The result is attractive as the flowers are lifted up and a downward flow can be obtained. However, it can be top-heavy if a lot of plant material is used and the smaller candlecups available are the most successful.

A candlecup is a metal or plastic dish with sides. A small knob underneath fits into the cavity of a candlestick or the neck of a bottle. It should be ringed with Plasticine before placing it in the bottle or candlestick. There is also a cavity in it, of the diameter of a candle, so that one may be placed among the flowers. The usual mechanics,

A grouping of plant material held in the hand and tied in position with a length of wool

These leaves have been cut short to hide the mechanics

Two stones used for covering a pinholder

Plasticine used to secure a candlecup in a candlestick

Mechanics placed in the candlecup

whichever are suitable, are used in the candlecup and it should be hidden with plant material.

Tube

Sometimes long-stemmed plant material is not available when needed. Tubes are sold which hold water and when attached with sticky tape to a square stick will lift flowers to a desired height, the stick and not the flower stem being pushed into the mechanics. This device is really only

A crosscut of wood makes a good base. A small piece of wood hides the well-type pinholder

suitable for large arrangements as the tube must be hidden with plant material.

Small tubes, such as those in which orchids are sold, may be used similarly for single flowers. They can also be pushed into a grouping of fruit or house plants to hold water for flowers.

Bases

This is the term used for anything on which the container stands. Bases are used extensively in flower arrangement and can add to the artistic appearance of the design and also protect the furniture from scratches and watermarks.

A collection of bases is useful and inexpensive as it can be employed in conjunction with well-type pinholders, as well as with decorative containers. One well-type pinholder and several bases will give a variety of effects without spending a lot of money.

Bases can be of any colour, size, texture, shape or substance to suit the plant material. Examples are oriental stands, trivets, pieces of slate, stone and marble, perspex, metal, crosscuts of wood,

14

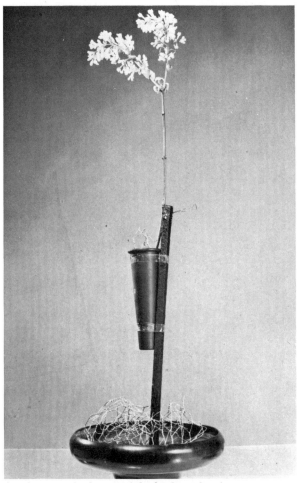

A tube, attached to a stick, for lengthening a stem

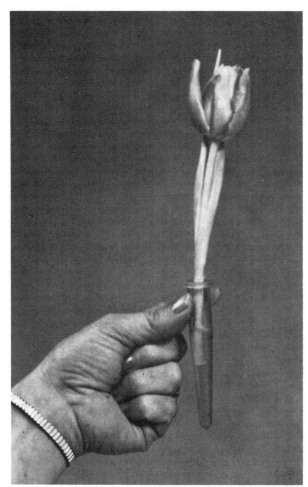

Small tubes are useful for holding water for one stem

bamboo, rush and straw mats. A useful base for a beginner in flower arrangement is made from a tray or cakeboard covered with fabric.

Method of making a base. Cut a piece of fabric to the shape of the board but with a two-inch margin all round. Turn in half an inch on the edge with an iron and then a further one inch. Stitch, leaving a small opening into which elastic can be slotted with a safety pin. Tighten and tie the ends of the elastic together and cut off any spare. This cover can then be slipped over the board or tray. It is easily removed for washing and a variety of slipcovers can be made for one board, giving different colours and textures.

Accessories

This term describes objects of non-plant material used in a design with plant material. It refers to things such as candles, figurines, jars and bottles which are not used as the container but added to the design for extra interest or to stretch the flowers when they are in short supply. Accessories

are not easy to incorporate into a design and it is wise to become reasonably accomplished in flower arrangement to begin with. But as interest grows it is fun to collect objects which can be combined with plant material attractively.

The equipment mentioned as basic is soon collected together without much expense. Further containers, bases and accessories can be collected as they are seen and as interest and knowledge grows. The search is continually fascinating.

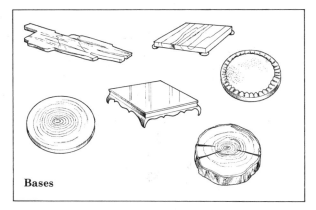

Bases

15

The Care of Cut Flowers and Foliage

A flower or leaf cut from a plant has a short, though beautiful life. It is possible to prolong this for a little while by a few simple methods. This is well worth doing as, having spent time and sometimes money on a flower arrangement, it is gratifying to have it last as long as possible.

Some flowers and leaves wilt before they reach the end of their normal lives but this can usually be avoided with a little care. Wilting occurs when a cut leaf or flower becomes short of water and these are often the causes:

1. It is not placed in water and there is no source to replace the supply which was given by the parent plant.
2. Although a source may be supplied by means of a bucket or container of water, the stem is not taking it up.
3. The stem end, when used in an arrangement, is not taking up enough water to replace the amount lost from the exposed leaves and flowers. This is because the air in a warm living room is much drier than the atmosphere of the garden where the plant material usually exists.

Flower arrangers use a collective term – *conditioning* – to refer to the preparation of cut plant material for a long life, the filling of stems with water and the prevention of wilt.

PREPARATION

All Flower Stems

1. Cut the stems on a slant.
2. Place the ends in water at once.
3. Re-cut any stems which have been left out of water, doing this under water if possible and removing about two inches of the stem.
4. Soak as much of the length of stem as is practical in deep warm water for about two hours before arranging in a room. This does not apply to florists' flowers.
Types of stem. In addition to the treatment just described, the following types of stem require further attention.

HARD STEMS. Cut upwards from the end for about one inch.
WOODY STEMS. Scrape off two inches of bark as well as cutting upwards.
HOLLOW STEMS. Fill with water and plug the end.
MILKY STEMS. Burn the stem end.

Foliage

Preparation is as follows:
1. Submerge all foliage (with the exception of grey leaves) under water for about two hours.
2. Remove from flower stems any foliage which might be under water when the flowers are arranged.
3. Remove all leaves from the stems of flowers which have shorter lives than most.

Damaged leaves should be removed before a stem is placed in an arrangement

Grooming

All plant material needs grooming before use. Foliage often needs washing – swishing in a sink of warm water is effective. Damaged leaves should be trimmed away. Bent stems and dead flowers should be cut off.

AFTERCARE

Place completed arrangements away from direct heat, sunlight and draughts. Top up the container with water when necessary. Add a mild disinfectant to the water to eliminate the need for changing it. Revive wilted flowers by re-cutting the stem end and submerging or floating the flower in water.

Briefly, these are the simple methods which help to prolong the lives of cut flowers and foliage. They do not take long and soon become habitual practice. The reasons for these methods are given later.

FLORISTS' FLOWERS

Florists' flowers travel and last well because they are grown specifically for the cut flower trade. No preparation should be necessary because this is done by the florist but, as the flowers will have been out of water during the journey home, it is wise to re-cut the stem ends. Preferably do this under water in a bucket and before making an arrangement. The normal two-hour soaking period for garden flowers can be omitted as this will have been given in the shop and the flowers may be arranged at once.

Good Buys

No florist knowingly sells old flowers but it is helpful to know the best buys and the signs which indicate age.

Buds. Many growers send flowers to market in tight bud, including the spring bulbous flowers, roses, gladioli, peonies and lilies. It is quite safe to buy these and they give more time for enjoyment of the flower. It is also interesting to watch them unfurl in your home.

Centres. The centres of young flowers are normally light yellow and the older ones are a darker gold. Loose pollen is an indication of a mature flower nearing the end of its life.

Foliage. The leaves on a flower stem should be crisp and bright in colour. Dry or brown leaves are an indication of old age. Wilting leaves are not old and soon recover when placed in water.

Stems. These should be green and not slimy or stained with brown patches.

Certain flowers have their own signs of youth to go by:

Chrysanthemums. Tightly curled petals at the centre and often a dimple or depression. Slightly drooping outer petals are of no concern.

Scabious. A light green and not a fluffy centre.

Carnations. A tight centre and firm outside petals.

Anthuriums. A light yellow centre.

Lilies and freesias. Glistening, firm and not crêpey petals.

Gladioli. The bottom flowers only show colour.

Florists' Long-lasting Flowers

The names are those normally used by the florist.

Achillea	Heather
Agapanthus	Ixia
Allium	Lily
Alstroemeria	Orchid
Anemone	Chincherinchee
Anthurium	Protea
Arum	Pyrethrum
Chrysanthemum	Rose, especially the
Clivia	varieties: Baccara (red)
Eremurus	and Carol (small, pink)
Eryngium	Straw Flower
Freesia	Strelitzia
Gladiolus	Sweet William
Gerbera	

GARDEN FLOWERS AND FOLIAGE

Many garden flowers, and in particular lilac, poppies and the old-fashioned roses, do not last long when cut. Most garden flowers have been cultivated for garden decoration and not for use in the house. Even so, they are lovely to look at in the home and this fleeting beauty is a great challenge – one is constantly trying to capture its charm. Gregory Conway, a skilled and famous flower arranger, wrote:

'The transient life of flowers is the very thing that gives expressiveness and interprets a philosophy of life'.

Garden flowers need more preparation than florists' flowers but it is well worthwhile and it begins at the time the flowers are cut in the garden.

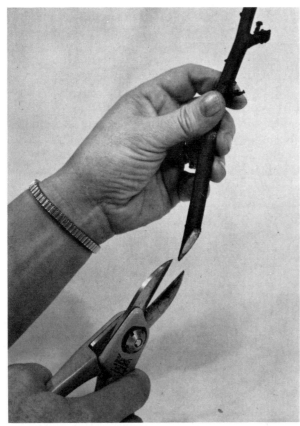

Cut stems on a slant for a better water intake

Cutting stems under water prevents the formation of air bubbles

Gathering Flowers

Time. In hot weather, gather flowers in the late evening. The heat of the sun reduces the water content during the middle of the day and the plant is likely to limp. In cooler or wet weather the plant material may be gathered at any time.

In the late evening the plant contains maximum food reserves which are made during the daylight hours and cells rich in these dissolved substances resist decay better. Cutting in the evening has yet another advantage – it gives the night-time for a long soak in water, so that the flowers are ready to arrange in the morning.

Method. Plant material should be out of water for as little time as possible and, romantic as a basket may look, it is better to take a bucket, half full of water, into the garden. The stems can then be put into water at once.

A plant consists of about nine-tenths water which distends the cells in the stem. When the water is withdrawn the cells collapse, the plant wilts and is no longer turgid (that is to say stiff and rigid due to a plentiful supply of water). The sources of water are the soil and the surrounding atmosphere so as soon as a stem is cut from the parent plant the main source of water is withdrawn. This must be replaced by another or air will enter the stem in its place. This is the reason for putting plant material into a bucket of water at once.

Stem Preparation

Cutting. When cutting from a plant, cut the stem on a slant as this exposes a greater surface of the inner tissue which takes in water more easily than the protective outside tissue.

Re-cutting. Stems which have not been placed in water immediately should be re-cut, removing about two inches from the ends. There are two reasons for this.

1. When the stem is cut from the parent plant, air enters the cut end. Sometimes this forms an air bubble which can prevent water travelling up the stem and causes wilting even though the stem may be standing in water. The air bubble can normally be removed by cutting off two inches of stem. If this second cut is made under water then no further air can enter the end.

2. When a stem is cut, the end begins to seal over (as with a cut finger) and a hard callus can form which does not allow water to enter the stem and again wilting will occur. Re-cutting removes the callus.

Soaking stems. Most flower stems benefit from standing in deep water for a minimum of two hours after the stem has received any other special preparation and before being arranged. This is because many plants can take a certain amount of water in through the whole length of the stem. This supplements the water entering the stem end and prepares the flower for a dry atmosphere. Flower, stem and leaf must be quite full of water because the amount taken in by the end of the stem does not always equal the amount lost in a dry room through the surface area of the exposed parts of the cutting. Gain of water from the container and loss of water to the air (transpiration) is always taking place, but not necessarily at an equal rate.

Stem types. Stems vary in their structure, which may be strong, weak, hard, soft and so on. Some stems take in and lose water more quickly than others. Some are supported by their turgidity (rigidity due to water distending the cells) alone and show signs of wilting quickly. This can make them more difficult for the flower arranger to use. Many wild flowers are examples. Other stems, such as holly, have rigid cell walls which, even when short of water, are strong enough to support the delicate tissues inside. Preparation of stems is dependent on the type of structure.

SOFT STEMS. These take in water easily and no further preparation other than re-cutting is necessary. The stems of spring bulbous flowers can become too soaked and floppy and are better arranged in shallow water, with only a short soaking period beforehand.

HARD STEMS. These take in water less easily and it is helpful to expose more of the inner softer tissue by cutting the stem upwards for one to two inches. Very thick stems can have more than one cut. Roses and chrysanthemums are examples of this type of stem.

WOODY STEMS. These have a really thick outer covering which is very protective and does not allow water to get in easily. About two inches of this covering should be scraped off the stem end with a knife, in addition to cutting the stem upwards. Lilac and cherry are examples.

HOLLOW STEMS. These may be upended and filled with water by means of a small funnel and a watering-can. Plug the end of the stem with cotton wool which will act as a wick, drawing more water into the centre of the stem when it is placed into a bucket.

Alternatively, the filled, hollow stem can be kept from leaking, when turned upright again, by placing a thumb over the end before putting it in the bucket of water for soaking. If the stem needs to be cut shorter for the final arrangement, cut under the water and place a thumb over the end,

After cutting soak the stems in a tall bucket

Cut hard stems upwards for impaling on a pinholder

Scrape the bark from woody stems for a length of 2 in.

19

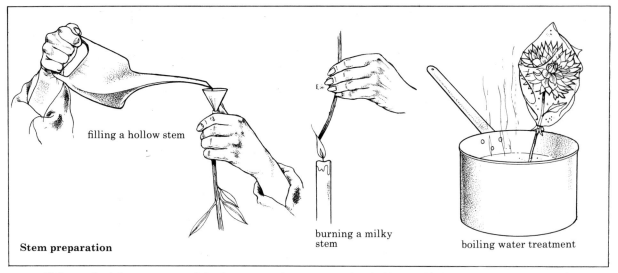

filling a hollow stem

burning a milky stem

boiling water treatment

Stem preparation

or stuff the end with cotton wool, before removing from the bucket. Filling the hollow stems seems to prevent premature falling of the flowers and water enters the stem more easily through the soft inside tissue than the protected outside. Lupins and delphiniums are examples.

MILKY STEMS. A few stems contain a milky substance – a solution of rubber called latex. This leaks out of the stem when it is cut and as it dries it hardens and forms a layer which prevents the intake of water. This leakage can be stopped by holding the stem end in the flame of a gas jet, candle or match, until it is blackened and stops sizzling. The cells are then killed at the cut surface and cannot leak the latex. Each time the stem is re-cut this process should be repeated. Euphorbias and poppies are examples.

WATER TEMPERATURE

Warm water. Most living processes take place better and faster at a warmer temperature. If warm water (that is of a temperature which is comfortably warm to the hands) is used for soaking the stems, it enters more easily and moves into the flowers and leaves more quickly. The water will cool in time but by then the stems should be full.

Boiling water. Excessive heat, such as from boiling water, kills cells subjected to it, but this can have several uses in conditioning:

1. The cut ends of stems are sterilised when held in the boiling water for a minute. The result is that the micro-organisms which are normally present and can produce slime to block the water channels, are reduced.

2. Dead cells at the stem ends cannot channel out sugars and other nutrients into the surrounding water. These solutions can also promote the growth of slime which prevents uptake of water.

3. Dead cells at the stem ends cannot grow into a callus which would seal the end and prevent water entering. However, re-cutting the stem is an easier method of removing a callus.

4. The heat expands any air in the stem which might be causing a blockage. Most of the air is forced out of the stem end in bubbles and replaced with water. However, this does not completely remove the air blockage and a more successful method is to re-cut the stem under water.

To summarise: boiling water is useful for sterilisation and preventing the loss of nutrients from the stems. It can also be of use in removing most of the air in an air blockage and in preventing the formation of a callus.

The method of treatment is to hold one inch of stem in boiling water for at least a minute. The stem can be left in the hot water until it cools. The flowers and foliage should be protected from hot steam with a cloth, paper or a polythene bag.

FOLIAGE

Leaves can take in water through their outside surface without damage. Push the foliage under warm water for a minimum of two hours. Young foliage should not be left longer or it deteriorates. It is always difficult to condition, beautiful as it may look, because the protective outer covering is not sufficiently developed and it loses water more quickly and wilts. More mature foliage may be left under water all night and will be full of water and crisp when removed in the morning.

Grey foliage. This should *not* be immersed as the grey effect is caused by many tiny hairs which become waterlogged and then appear green. These hairs can also drip water on to the furniture. It is better to place only the stem ends in water.

Removal of Foliage from Stems

1. Leaves growing from the lower part of the flower stems may end up under water when the flowers are arranged. It is better to remove them or they decay.

2. Some flowers, which normally have a short life, last longer if all the foliage is removed from the stem. The transpiring surfaces are then cut down and all available water goes into the flowers. Clematis and lilac are examples.

3. Some plants have good flowers but foliage that wilts easily. In this case the leaves should be removed and other foliage used with the flowers. Achillea and amaranthus are examples.

4. Foliage with damaged edges can be trimmed with flower scissors.

Condition foliage by soaking it in water for two hours

AFTERCARE OF ARRANGEMENTS

Placement

The position in which the flower arrangement is placed in a room can effect the length of life of the plant material. Whenever possible it should be placed away from the direct heat of a fire, lamp, television set or strong sunshine, all of which cause rapid transpiration. Draughts have the same effect. The coolest place in a room is the best one for a long life. If necessary remove an arrangement that you wish to last well to a cooler place overnight.

Topping up with Water

Plastic foam and small containers should be topped up daily with water, especially if they are in a drying atmosphere or contain many flowers. Spraying plant material with water increases the humidity of the surrounding air – but can mark the furniture. Again, arrangements which are especially required to last well may be removed to a cool place overnight and sprayed to increase the humidity.

Water change. Many flowers do not live long enough to produce really contaminated water but some long-lasting flowers, such as chrysanthemums, can make water smell unpleasant. This and water changing can be avoided by adding a mild disinfectant. Experiments in hospitals, made to save work for the nurses, have proved that a quarter of a teaspoonful of chlorhexidine to one pint of water is effective.

Additives to water. There are many old wives' tales about such things as pennies, aspirin and gin lengthening the life of cut flowers. There are also

A spray of lilac defoliated to avoid water loss

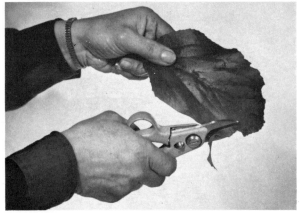
Trimming the edge from a piece of damaged foliage

21

A small watering-can is used to top up an arrangement with water. This may be necessary each day

22

modern commercial mixtures sold for this purpose. However, there is no substitute for good conditioning before the flowers are arranged and nothing appears to make a remarkable difference to the length of life. The best advice is to test each idea for yourself if you have the inclination. What works for one person may not work for another because of differences in the composition of tap water, the mixing of ingredients, the stage at which the plant material is picked or bought and the surrounding atmosphere.

Wilted Flowers

There is a difference between a wilted flower and a dead one. The dead flower has reached the end of its life but a wilted flower is only short of water. For some reason the stem is not taking up the water provided. Often it can be revived with 'first-aid' treatment. Take the wilted flower out of the arrangement and try one of the following methods:

1. Re-cut the stem under water, removing about two inches. Leave in deep warm water for two hours.
2. Float the entire flower and stem in water after re-cutting. This works well with roses and other flowers which may wilt with a bend at the top of the stem.
3. Defoliate the stem, re-cut it and submerge the flower and stem in water for about an hour. If left for longer the delicate tissues of flower petals may become damaged. This method suits flowers such as clematis which are always hard to condition.
4. Re-cut the stem and place in one inch of boiling water. Leave to cool. This works when the wilt is more general and not only at the top of the stem.

SPECIAL TREATMENT

Experience has taught that some flowers respond to special treatment in conditioning before they can appear at their best. These requirements are listed below.

Alliums. Avoid using hot water as it increases the onion smell.

Berries. Spray with clear varnish or hair lacquer for some protection from shrivelling.

Bougainvilleas. Submerge overnight.

Bulrushes. Spray with hair lacquer or clear varnish to prevent 'blowing'.

Camellias. Spray often with water as the hard woody stems do not take in water easily.

Chincherinchees. Cut off the waxed ends used

Spraying with water helps to increase the humidity

Although in bud the flower on the right is wilting from lack of water

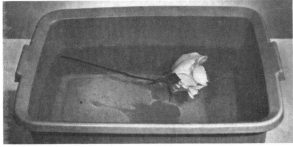

Floating a rose in water increases its water content

23

for transportation before soaking the stems.

Clematis. Defoliate and submerge the flowers for an hour.

Coleus foliage. Do not submerge as the leaves become transparent.

Edelweiss. Keep the flowers well above the water as it spoils the colour.

Gardenias. The flowers mark easily and should be handled very little and with wet hands.

Gerberas. An air bubble is common so cut off at least 2 in. of the stems under water.

Gladioli. These can be retarded very well in the bud stage by leaving out of water in a cool place for several days.

Hellebores. These last much longer in the fruit stage. If picked earlier they last better when arranged in deep water.

Hibiscus. These are short-lived and last as well out of water as in water.

Hippeastrums. Last well in little water but need a stick in the hollow stems for support.

Holly berries. These are often eaten by birds before Christmas unless picked about three weeks earlier. Place the branches in a bucket half-full of water. Put a polythene bag over the top and tuck it into the sides of the bucket. The berries are protected and become very plump. The bucket may be left outside to keep cool.

Hydrangeas. The 'petals' are flower-like bracts and may be submerged, as foliage, for up to two hours. If wilting occurs when the stems are in the arrangement, they can often be revived by placing damp tissue paper over the 'flowers' to increase the humidity. Alternatively spray well with water.

Kale. Avoid hot water which increases the 'cooking cabbage' smell.

Laburnum. Defoliate.

Lilies. Remove the anthers with flower scissors as the pollen can stain clothes.

Mimosa. Keep in a polythene bag until immediately before arranging. Spray with water.

Molucella laevis (Bells of Ireland). Defoliate.

Pelargoniums (Geraniums). Spray the back of the flowers with hair lacquer to hold the petals on longer.

Peonies. These may be retarded in the bud stage by leaving out of water in a cool place. Re-cut the stems and place in warm water to start development again.

Philadelphus. Defoliate.

Phytolacca americana (American Pokeberry). Handle carefully to avoid berries staining clothing.

Poinsettias. The ends must be charred as these are euphorbias and have milky stems.

Sansevieria. The leaves become soggy in water.

Polythene should be wrapped around the stem ends in an arrangement. They can be used out of water without becoming wilted.

Stephanotis. The flowers can turn brown if touched by water.

Strelitzias. The individual petals may be eased out of the sheath if they do not appear gradually.

Sweet peas. Handle as little as possible.

Tulips. Straighter stems can result from wrapping in newspaper during the soaking period.

Violets. A damp atmosphere is needed so submerge now and again, or spray with water.

Water lilies. To hold the petals open drop melted wax around the centre.

Zinnias. A wire pushed up the hollow stems prevents the stems from bending over.

Forcing Branches

Flowering branches can be induced to flower earlier than normal by receiving extra warmth. This is successful with trees and shrubs which flower in the spring:

Almond	Jasmine
Apple	Lilac
Black currant	Magnolia
Cherry	Peach
Forsythia	Pear
Hazel	Plum
Honeysuckle	Willow
Japanese quince	

Method. Cut branches when large buds appear and there are good signs of life. The flowers open more rapidly the closer it is to the normal time of flowering. Scrape 2 in. of bark away from the stem end of a branch and place it in boiling water for at least a minute. Leave it in the water in a warm place. Change the water often, replacing with warm water.

Retarding Flowers

The development of flowers can be retarded in a refrigerator. This is suitable for flowers with strong stems such as roses, carnations, tulips and chrysanthemums, which may be held back for up to a week. It is useful if flowers are needed at different stages of development for a special event. Open roses can result from being left in a warm room, half-open flowers from a cool room and buds from being kept in a refrigerator. In hot countries flowers may be kept in a refrigerator until needed for an arrangement – and are often bought from a refrigerator in the florist's shop.

Method. Soak the stem for the normal two hours

and then tie the whole flower into a polythene bag and place in the refrigerator until wanted. For short periods flowers may be placed in a jug of water. Short-stemmed flowers, such as orchids, can be placed in boxes with lids. Miniature arrangements being prepared for show work may be similarly treated.

There is still much to be discovered about the conditioning and keeping of cut plant material. It is expected that because of experiments being conducted by individuals and commercial concerns great strides will be made in the next few years.

TRANSPORTING FLOWERS

Florists' flowers. These should be wrapped in paper with the flowers protected to prevent damage from hot sun, wind, draughts and cold.
Garden flowers. In cool weather these can be carried in a polythene bag to conserve moisture. In hot weather this causes rapid development and petals also become damaged. A cardboard box is better in this case.
Wild flowers. If possible place them immediately into a bucket of water. If this is not possible, a polythene bag which must be kept out of the sun can be a substitute. They wilt quickly if not kept moist and are difficult to revive.

Packing

For long journeys and for mailing pack the flowers in a cardboard box without polythene. Let the flowers support each other but see that the flower heads are not on top of each other. At a florist's shop look at the way flowers are packed for transporting by the grower. Small sticks are often placed across the stems to hold them in place.
Specimen flowers. Growers usually pack very special flowers such as orchids and anthuriums with each stem in a small tube of water. These tubes are useful for packing your own special flowers for long journeys. They can also be used for inserting a few flowers in arrangements of fruit or in a group of house plants. Similarly, water may be placed in deflated balloons which can be tied to stem ends.
Foliage. Leaves are not damaged, as are flowers, by being carried in a polythene bag, even in hot weather. Tough leaves last many days kept in a bag. Tie up the open end to hold in the moisture.
Spike-shaped flowers. If kept in a horizontal position for several hours, these tend to curl

Chrysanthemums packed for travelling in a cardboard box. Rolls of corrugated paper support the flower heads

upwards at the tips. Sometimes this is desirable but otherwise carry them upright or with the tips lightly held down with a stick or tied together. This applies to such flowers as delphiniums and larkspurs.
Complete arrangements. Arrangements in tall containers may be transported upright by placing them in a deep wide cardboard box with newspaper packed tightly around the container for support. Arrangements in low containers travel well placed on the floor of the car.

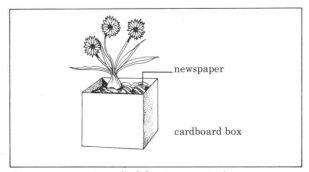

An arrangement packed for transportation

Arranging Flowers

How should you arrange the beautiful flowers that you pick or buy for your home? It is thought by some people that there are definite rules which must be followed, but this is not true. 'Rules' only apply to competitive work in flower arrangement shows. Some people also think that a flower arrangement must conform to a set pattern, use certain shapes or a definite number of flowers, and so on. Again this is not true and the only things of concern are that:

1. The beauty of the flowers is well displayed and any remarkable quality, such as a vibrant colour or a lovely curve, is clearly seen.
2. The arrangement complements your home and adds to its attraction.
3. The actual job of arranging is enjoyed as a happy, creative activity.

As soon as the methods of supporting stems in a container and of conditioning flowers and leaves are understood, flower arrangement can begin. There are a few guide lines which can help the

Scale: The tulips are of a similar size but the container on the left is too big, the middle one is too small. The container on the right is a better size

beginner to choose plant material in the flower shop or garden and to arrange it in a container of water.

SELECTION OF PLANT MATERIAL

Restraint

Choosing the right plant material in the first place is half the battle. Most people start by buying or picking far too much and then, quite naturally, feel that it must go into the arrangement. This clutters up the design and over-crowding is one of the biggest faults. Beautiful objects look so much better when well displayed with space around them to show their form. A sculpture looks wonderful set against the open sky and a single dress is noticed and admired far more than many dresses cluttered together in a shop window. And so it is with flowers – space and restraint are essential for displaying their beauty. It is wise to pick or buy *less* than you think you will need for an arrangement.

Number of Varieties

Choose only a few varieties of plant material when you begin flower arrangement – perhaps one type of flower and one type of foliage. This means that you can concentrate on enhancing their special beauty without being confused by the various qualities of colour, texture and shape of many flowers. How to combine several varieties is something to be learnt gradually as you become more advanced.

Size

When you pick or buy think of the sizes of everything. The different pieces of plant material should relate to each other in size, to give a feeling of belonging to each other. For example, a large hydrangea flower and the leaf of a violet look incongruous together and it is better to choose flowers and leaves closer to each other in size.

1. The container is too important. Use: 2. Taller material 3. Larger material 4. More material

The plant material should also relate in size to the container, otherwise it will either appear to dominate the container or it will be overwhelmed by it. Size relationship is called *scale*.

Colours

Choose colours which you feel suit each other and the container which is also a part of the design. The final result should be a pleasing whole and not a design of two separate parts – the plant material and the container. The dull earthy colours, browns, greys, greens, which are easy to blend with flower colours are good for containers. Brighter colours and white are more difficult. White is successful if some white can be seen in the plant material to provide a link, and the same applies to black containers. For example, the colour is repeated when a tulip is used with a black centre.

The colours of the flowers should also suit the room in which they are to be placed so that the room and the flower arrangement appear co-ordinated.

To summarise – the guide lines when selecting plant materials are:
1. Restrain buying or picking so that each flower can be displayed well.
2. Use fewer varieties when beginning to learn flower arrangement, to avoid a confused appearance.
3. Relate the plant material and container in scale.
4. Suit the colours of the plant material and container to each other.

ARRANGING FLOWERS

The following points are helpful whatever the style of design.

Space

Shape cannot be defined without the use of space. Each piece of plant material can only be clearly seen if it is in its own space and not bunched against other flowers and leaves. Styles of flower arrangement vary and some use many flowers and leaves and allow little space between them while others have little plant material and larger spaces in between – but to some extent space is necessary in all styles.

Importance

It is usual for the plant material to appear more important than the container. The container is necessary to hold water and the stem ends but it should show off the beauty of the flowers and not compete with them for attention. When the container seems to look more important try (another time) using taller, larger, or a greater quantity of plant material to offset this.

Turning Flowers

Turn flowers to face in different directions. The back and sides of a flower are often as beautiful as the front. Turning flowers gives more interest and variety and looks natural, because flowers growing on a plant usually turn in all directions. The flower paintings of the Dutch and Flemish Old Masters are wonderful examples, well worth studying, of flowers being seen at all angles.

Length of Stem

There is more interest if flowers are seen on stems of different lengths. This also eliminates a top-

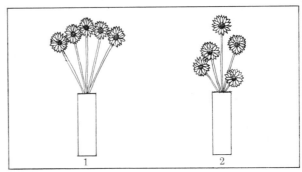

1. Stems of equal length 2. Stems of unequal length

27

Flowers can be beautiful from all angles

The stems on the left radiate from a central point

heavy appearance, which may be given when the stems are all the same length, and helps to separate each flower head so that it can be seen clearly.

Radiation

There is a greater sense of rhythm and 'flow' if the stem ends are centred closely together in the mechanics. Radiation from a central point is quite natural. Many plants grow up through the ground with a single stem which then divides in every

direction to receive light and rain. Look at winter trees for lovely examples. Radiation can also be seen in many forms of art such as the fan-vaulting of cathedral roofs.

To summarise – the guide lines for use when arranging most styles of flower arrangement are:
1. Allow space around each flower.
2. Make the plant material more important than the container.
3. Turn the flower heads to face different directions.
4. Cut the stems to different lengths.
5. Keep the stem ends close together.

Making a Start

When you begin arranging flowers the first attempts are very likely to be faltering – this happens when learning anything that is new. Confidence, however, builds up and practice soon makes arranging flowers quick and easy. When you are ready to begin an arrangement:
1. 'Clear the decks' – sufficient space in which to work and to see the arrangement as it grows is essential.
2. Sit down if at all possible – it is more relaxing.
3. Hold each piece of plant material approximately in the position you think it will occupy before you cut a stem to see if you like it.
4. Make sure that the plant material is always firmly supported as wobbly mechanics can be disconcerting.

MAKING A SIMPLE ARRANGEMENT (PRACTICAL ARRANGEMENT 1)

It is helpful to begin with a design which uses only a few pieces of plant material.

COMPONENTS
(A) Baking dish for the container – about 12 in. long, in a dull colour.
(B) 3-in. pinholder and Plasticine for holding it securely in place.
(C) Flower scissors.
(D) 2 flowers of the same variety such as roses or medium-sized chrysanthemum blooms. These may be in different stages of development, with stems about 11 in. long.
(E) 2 or 3 leaves of the same variety, in good condition, such as hosta or large ivy.
(F) 2 branches with woody stems. The simplest are those without leaves or with *most* of the foliage removed. Choose branches which have an in-

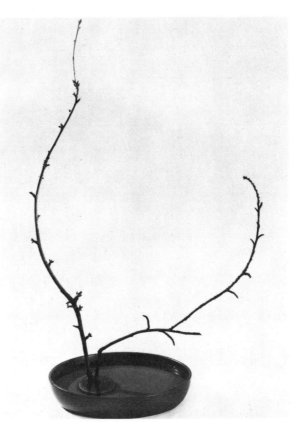

Practical Arrangement I: The first branch is placed on the pinholder

The second branch is positioned with its base close to that of the first

teresting shape. They should be about 22 in. long.
(G) Small sheet of polythene, or a cardboard box, on which to drop the rubbish.
(H) 2 or 3 stones for hiding the pinholder.
(I) Watering-can (small).

METHOD
1. Condition the plant material and wash the leaves if they are dirty. Trim off any damaged or unwanted leaves.
2. Fix the pinholder in the container.
3. Pour water into the container until it covers the pinholder.
4. Place the plant material in position. It does not matter which piece of plant material is placed on the pinholder first but it is usually easier to start with the branches as they are the larger.

Push one branch firmly on to the pinholder at the centre back and then gently press it down so that it leans to one side – this leaves room for other plant material. It may be necessary to cut up the stem end with flower scissors to get it on to the pinholder more easily. It is helpful if the tip of the branch turns inwards towards the centre of the design and not outwards, which can carry the eyes away and out of the arrangement.

Place the second branch, cut a little shorter and pruned if necessary, with its stem end very close to the stem end of the first branch on the pinholder. Bend gently into a position where it may be clearly seen and is not confused with the first branch.

The length of the branches does not matter to the nearest inch and measuring accurately is not compatible with an art such as flower arrangement. The only consideration is that the plant material should look more important than the container when the design is complete. A rough guide is to cut the tallest branch to a length which is at least 1½ times the width of the baking dish.

Before arranging, the second branch was trimmed in two places to give a better shape

Two chrysanthemums are added for interest. These are placed near together but at different heights

As the design seems rather bare, two honesty leaves are added to soften the effect

When a container is used which is greater in height than in width, cut the branch at least 1½ times the *height* and not the width.

The eye is a good judge, however, and if the branch seems too long and heavy and to dominate the container unduly, then shorten it. If it seems very fine and slender for the container, then leave it longer.

Add the two flowers, placed near together, at different heights, in any space that is now left, keeping the stem ends close together on the pinholder. For good balance position the flower heads approximately halfway between the tip of the tallest branch and the bottom of the container.

If the design seems stark, add the leaves but omit them if the arrangement seems complete without them. Again, place the stem ends together on the pinholder and the leaves at slightly different angles.

5. If the pinholder shows, hide it by placing the stones over it.
6. Position the arrangement in a room and top up the container with water, using the watering-can to ensure that none is spilt.
7. Look at the arrangement often in the next few

days. Study the way you have placed the material and decide if you can try a different placement another time.

Similar Arrangements

There are many positions in which plant material may be placed even when only a few pieces are used in the design. Practise different positions with the same container and mechanics and similar plant material – that is branches, flowers and leaves (perhaps of other varieties). Try using three branches instead of two. Try using various lengths of plant material and see which you prefer. Study also the spaces which you create as you add each piece of plant material to the design. Decide how *little* you need for a design remembering the importance of restraint in the choice of material.

This style can also be created with bases and well-type pinholders to give a great variety of effects. It is very suitable for winter when flowers are scarce and expensive. It is also suitable for someone starting flower arrangement who may be confused at first by trying to arrange larger quantities of plant material.

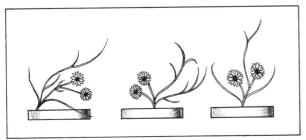

Several different arrangements can be composed from similar plant material

SHAPES OF PLANT MATERIAL

The arrangement just described uses three shapes which can be defined as *basic* – linear, round and a shape in-between the round and the linear. Very generally speaking all plant material can be classified in this way. Each of these shapes plays a different part in a design.

Linear shapes, or lines as they are usually called, move the eyes along and do not hold them in one place. Notice how your eyes go up and down the lines.

Round or near-round shapes, which in design terms are called 'points', tend to hold the eyes and give them a short rest.

In-between shapes do not either hold the eye strongly or move it along rapidly. Their role in a design is as a peacemaker between the other two shapes and they make the arrangement appear less stark. These shapes can also be called stepping stones.

When you have made one of the simple arrangements previously described, look at the shapes used in it. The lines (branches) draw the eyes into the design giving a path to follow. The flowers,

which are rounds, hold the eyes and give a resting place, and the in-between shapes (leaves) act as stepping stones or 'softeners'.

The flowers may be likened to the 'star performers' in a production and are the centre of attraction, holding the eye longer than anything else. The branches, leaves and container are the supporting actors, who help the stars to be well displayed.

LINE AND MASS ARRANGEMENTS

Styles in flower arrangement fall generally into one of two broad classifications – line and mass. The characteristics of each are given.

Line

(A) Lines are an important feature of the design.
(B) Restraint is used in the amount of plant material – because then the lines can be seen clearly.
(C) There is a lot of space within the design itself, again so that the lines can be seen clearly.
(D) The beauty of the design lies in the individual qualities of each piece of plant material.

This restrained line arrangement shows the beauty of the apple blossom

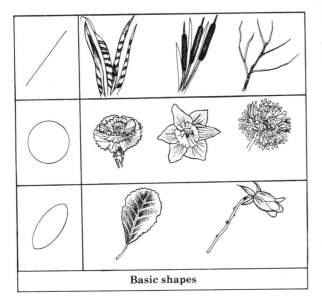

Basic shapes

31

Mass

(A) Few lines can be seen and more use is made in the design of rounded and in-between shapes.
(B) There is a sense of full, massed beauty and not of restraint.
(C) Little space is used within the design.
(D) The interest is not so much in the individual beauty of each piece of plant material but in the bouquet effect of massed colours, shapes and textures.
(E) The external outline is solid and emphasised and is often a recognisable geometric shape such as a circle, oval or triangle.

Both these styles are beautiful but in different ways. Line designs, which originated in the East where space has long been a valued quality, are economical in winter. Mass designs, more characteristic of the West, are suitable for the summer when flowers are more plentiful.

Massed-line or Line-mass

This is the term given to describe designs which have the characteristics of both line and mass and do not fit clearly into either the line or mass classifications. In other words there is a strong

A massed-line arrangement using chrysanthemums, beech leaves and driftwood

sense of line but also a mass of plant material somewhere in the design. This style originated in America.

A SIMPLE MASS ARRANGEMENT (PRACTICAL ARRANGEMENT 2)

The first practical arrangement can be classified as a *line* arrangement because of the important branches which are called line plant material. The next style to practise is a *mass* arrangement which suits traditional homes and is useful as a centrepiece for a table at mealtimes. It is also an excellent way of providing a strong accent of colour in a room.

The simplest mass arrangement and one that has been used for centuries is the bouquet or nosegay style, in which the flowers are placed close together in a rounded design. It is not difficult to arrange and the effect is of massed colour and texture with the outline of the design being more emphasised than the shape of each flower. It has a heavier appearance than a line arrangement, which uses more space within the design, and it can also look rather static as the many rounded shapes attract and hold the eye and there is less movement. This can be lessened by turning the flowers around an imaginary central axis so that they are not all seen full face.

Plastic foam is the easiest method of support and a stemmed container lightens the heaviness of the design. It is again helpful to start arranging this style using only one variety of flower and one of foliage until there has been plenty of practice in the placement of plant material.

COMPONENTS
(A) Stemmed container with a bowl-shaped receptacle for the flowers.
(B) Block of plastic foam – more than half the big block normally sold should rarely be necessary.
(C) Plastic foam pinholder and Plasticine to hold it firmly.
(D) Wire netting (1-in. mesh) which will be needed for a 'cap' over the foam if it stands well out of the container or seems wobbly.
(E) Wire from a reel to tie the netting to the container.
(F) Flower scissors.
(G) Approximately 8 flowers such as roses or marguerites with stems varying from 6 to 8 in. long. The flowers may be of differing sizes and stages of development to give greater interest.
(H) Approximately 6 leaves such as rose, small hosta or ivy, remembering that they should be in

A simple mass arrangement of the rose Magenta in an Art Nouveau container. The flowers are turned to face different ways and the stems are of differing heights

scale with the flowers chosen for the design.
(I) Small sheet of polythene or a cardboard box on which to drop the rubbish.
(J) Watering-can.

METHOD
1. Condition, clean and trim the plant material.
2. Soak the plastic foam and secure it in the container with the pinholder and wire netting if desired.
3. Place the plant material in position. Start where you like, however, it is often easier to place some of the leaves in position to cover the plastic foam before putting in flowers. Cut the stems very short and place each leaf so that it is almost flat against the foam. This not only helps to hide the foam but also gives a dense background which shows off the flowers well. Add the flowers, lifting the leaves if necessary to insert the stems. Remember the guide lines suggested: leave a little space around each flower; make the flowers appear more important than the container; turn the flower heads to face different ways; cut stems of slightly differing lengths, placing shorter stems close to the foam and the longer ones further out. This gives an in-and-out appearance which is called recessing. It is more pleasing than a mass arrangement of flowers which have stems all of the same length.

There can still be a sense of radiation from a central point when using plastic foam although the stem ends cannot be seen. It is helpful to imagine them almost meeting in the centre of the foam (although it is not necessary for the ends to be placed right into the centre).
4. Turn the design to see that the outline is more or less even. A turntable is useful and one normally used for icing cakes or placing on the table at meal times can be bought inexpensively at an ironmonger's shop.
5. See that the foam is covered and, if necessary, add more leaves, tucking them into the design.

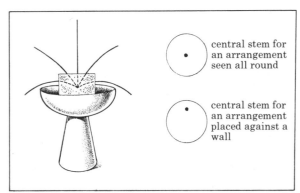

The stem ends are positioned in the foam to achieve a sense of radiation

6. Place the arrangement in a room and fill the container with water if possible. If not remember to add a little water on top of the plastic foam each day as the surface can dry out.

Length of stem. If the arrangement is to be seen all round and is used for a table arrangement when people are seated for a meal, the centre stem should be placed in the middle of the plastic foam and kept low so that it does not interfere with conversation across the table.

If the arrangement is to be placed against a wall and not seen all round, then the centre stem should be placed about two-thirds of the way back on the foam and it can be taller, giving more of an oval effect than a circular one.

Depth. Less plant material may be placed at the back of an arrangement which is positioned against a wall as it is not so easily seen. However, it is surprising how flowers placed at the back can be seen from the front. This also gives greater interest especially if the flower points backwards so that its back is seen. It also gives an impression of depth and good radiation which is both attractive and natural.

A plant stem often appears growing from the ground with the growth dividing in all directions and radiating from this central stem. The backs and sides of the flowers are seen turning around the central stem. A flower arrangement can have the flowers turning around an imaginary central axis in the same way.

Similar Mass Arrangements

Practise simple mass designs such as this using, if available, other containers and different varieties of flowers and leaves. Keep to one variety until you are confident of the placement and can easily accomplish a pleasing shape. Then start to mix varieties of flowers, leaves, seed heads and berries using several colours, shapes and textures, always bearing in mind the basic guide lines summarised on page 28.

A MASS DESIGN WITH TRIANGULAR
FRAMEWORK – (PRACTICAL
ARRANGEMENT 3)

This is a classical style which has always been popular. Instead of following a rounded or oval outline, the framework is triangular. Although the term triangle is used to describe this style by flower arrangers, it is not two dimensional as one drawn on a piece of paper, but is three dimensional with little flatness anywhere. However, if the

A triangular arrangement of sprays of prunus with pink camellias

Above: A china figurine used as an accessory in a design of garden flowers, wild flowers and foliage on a fabric-covered base. Accessories should be integrated into the design

Opposite: A triangular arrangement of garden flowers, including bocconia, poppy seed heads, stocks, roses, onopordum, sedum and lilies, in an antique Persian candlestick

silhouette or shadow of the design could be seen it would give a triangular appearance.

COMPONENTS

(A) A container with a stem, if possible, as this enables plant material to flow downwards at the sides.

(B) Plant material that includes two or three large round flowers, smaller flowers and leaves. All the plant material should be related in size and colour.

(C) Mechanics for the container. Plastic foam or a pinholder with wire netting are more suitable than a pinholder alone which cannot hold a great quantity of plant material.

(D) A base, if desired.

METHOD

1. Condition the plant material and fix the mechanics in the container.

2. This style is not suitable for an all-round design in the centre of a table because of its high top point. It is normally placed in front of a wall. There are no rules about beginning but it is easier to position the tallest stems (which may belong to a leaf or a small flower) first, two-thirds of the way back on the mechanics. This gives the top point of the triangle, often called the backbone. This stem should be roughly 1½ times the height of the container but it depends on the type of plant material and the visual weight of the container. A brightly coloured or highly decorated container will need taller plant material to help offset the strong attraction created by the colour or the decoration.

Place two stems of roughly equal length at the sides of the design. A better appearance is given if these are shorter than the top stem. These complete the three points of the triangle and all other plant material is kept to the imaginary lines which these three points suggest as an outline. The appearance of the design is softer and more rhythmic if the 'arms' are formed with curved plant material such as ivy. The straighter plant material is more suitable for the backbone.

The arrangement will be very flat at the back and front unless depth is added. This can be done by adding shorter plant material low in the design pointing towards the back and towards the front. All three dimensions have now been outlined – height, width and depth.

3. Keeping within the framework, add other plant material. The balance is better and there is more rhythm if the bigger flowers are placed at the centre of the design. This is often called the centre of interest and its position should roughly be halfway between the bottom of the container (or base if used) and the top point of the design, for good balance.

4. Add foliage placed closely against the foam to cover it.

5. Add other plant material, keeping to the framework. A good sense of rhythm results from having smaller flowers around the outside of the centre of interest gradually changing in size to the smallest flowers which are used on the outside of the design. Remember the basic guide lines of allowing space around each flower, a gradual turning of the flowers around an imaginary central axis, and having stems of different lengths radiating from a central point.

OTHER DESIGNS

Examples of three practical arrangements have now been given – one line and two mass designs. The latter are classical designs which are always popular. These, however, should not be rigidly and regularly repeated. Plant material can be arranged in any way you like and inspiration can be found from the way plants grow and from other forms of art.

Experimentation is essential and fun. This is what makes flower arrangement so fascinating – one continually tries new things to find out the limits and possibilities of the plant material. You should not worry if the results are not always to your own or other peoples' liking. Great artists have not always produced masterpieces and when they have, the results are often the fruits of many hours of trial and error.

THE MEDIUM OF PLANT MATERIAL

There are many different types of plant material to try out and to combine – driftwood, roots, bark,

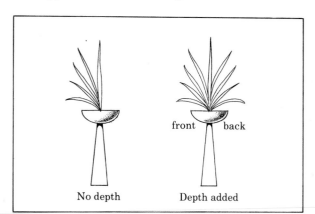

No depth   Depth added

Side-view of an arrangement showing shorter plant material added to obtain a three-dimensional effect

branches, tree stumps, crosscuts of tree trunks, berries, fruits, seed heads, cones, fungus, vegetables, flowers, leaves and stems. They can be fresh or preserved, and wild or cultivated, but all are interesting.

The term 'flower arrangement', which is very inadequate, suggests that flowers should always be present in a design. This is limiting and unnecessary – but no better name for an art which uses the medium of plant material has yet been invented. There are many wonderful designs without flowers – arrangements of foliage, bark, driftwood, seed heads, branches, fruit and so on, and sometimes the addition of flowers is superfluous and can spoil the effect.

Working with Plant Material

Artists should know the possibilities and limitations of the material with which they work if they are to be successful. Getting to know flowers, leaves, branches and so on is as important to a flower arranger as an artist knowing about the possibilities of paint and a potter of clay.

Plant material is not as malleable as paint, clay and even needlework thread. It has its own way of growing and is too fragile to be changed very much by the flower arranger without the delicate tissues being spoiled. Flower arrangement is not an art of changing the material into new forms but an art of assembling materials with colours, textures and shape into a pleasing whole.

A lot of plant material looks better arranged according to its natural habit of growth. For example, a dignified gladiolus looks better arranged upright as it grows in the garden rather than placed on its side unnaturally and as though blown down by the wind. Curved stems can seldom be straightened, and look better where softness is desirable, whereas straight stems can rarely be made to bend and should be used when a straight effect is needed.

Playing with the material. Play with the plant material before placing it in the container. This means looking closely at each piece and observing its qualities, combining it with other materials in your hand to see which are pleasing together and so on. Having played for a while and decided more or less how to use the plant material then start making the arrangement.

The importance of speed. Place the plant material in position quickly. Changing the position again and again does not usually help and everything begins to look tired, including the arranger. The transient life of cut plant material does not justify a long time being taken over one

Gladioli arranged in a dignified manner in a pottery container. Stones hide the pinholder

arrangement and rarely is it improved by 'labouring'. Short-lived plant material has one great advantage – a poor flower arrangement does not last as long as a poor book or painting.

It is advisable to arrange quickly after the initial playing and leave the design unaltered even if faults are seen later. If you start making one alteration others usually follow and this upsets the whole design. It is much better to leave the fault, which you will consciously correct the next time you make an arrangement.

Knowing when to stop. It is very easy to put too much into an arrangement. This clutters up the design and the ordered, simple effect is easily lost. Stop when the design seems to be 'jelling' and you are not quite sure where to place the next piece of plant material. Then look at the arrangement and see if anything can be removed. A good design is one in which everything is needed.

Above: Grey foliage and flowers of onopordum with gerbera daisies. It is important not to wet this foliage as it spoils the grey effect
Opposite: Windscreen glass hides the pinholder in a simple arrangement of magnolia branches. Woody stems should be scraped and split before use

Any spare piece of plant material may be used in another arrangement, or can be popped into a jam jar by the sink where it can be continually observed and the beauty of its individual qualities seen – the centre of the flower, the curve of a stem, the texture of a leaf, the symmetry of the petals and so on. This helps you to understand the medium of plant material and to enhance its qualities when you arrange it.

ASSESSING YOUR DESIGNS

Assessment of your designs is important if you are to improve. However, it may be very difficult to assess your own flower arrangements and a teacher or knowledgeable friend can often point out something that could be improved. It is also surprising how a non-flower-arranging member of the family can put a finger on a major fault that you may have missed, such as 'The leaves look too big for the flowers', or 'the design looks all container'.

It is not always possible to have a teacher or friend available and it then becomes necessary for you to assess your own work. One way of doing this is to go away immediately after completing the arrangement and forget it. Then, when you have a little time, sit down and study the design, asking yourself the following questions to help assessment.

1. Are the mechanics firm or wobbly?
2. Are the mechanics hidden?
3. Do the flowers look fresh and well groomed?
4. Is the container the correct size for the arrangement?
5. Do the individual pieces of plant material suit each other in size?
6. Do the colours of the plant material and the container suit each other?
7. Does the container seem to be a separate part of the design or does it appear as a 'whole' design *with* the plant material?
8. Is everything clearly seen in space or is it overcrowded?
9. Are my eyes equally attracted to both sides of the design giving a sense of balance?
10. Do all the parts of the design – container, base, plant material – appear to belong to each other?
11. Are some flowers turned so that different parts are seen?
12. Do the stems appear to radiate from a central point?
13. Can anything be removed from the design and not be missed?
14. Did I enjoy arranging the flowers?

Preserving Plant Material

There are certain times of the year, such as the winter months in the British Isles and the hot summers in America and other parts of the world, when fresh plant material is scarce or in poor condition. It is frustrating to give up arranging flowers at these times, but this is not at all necessary if plant material is preserved when plentiful. There are several methods of preservation and in many cases the results last for years and may be used again and again.

Preserved plant material can be arranged in containers either on its own or combined with fresh plant material. It can be made into permanent or semi-permanent decorations for the home. In addition to being used in arrangements, it can be made into plaques, swags and pressed flower pictures. It is also useful for Christmas decorations as it can be sprayed with metallic paints and glittered.

The methods of preservation fall into two main categories.
First, drying by:
Hanging up.
Pressing under a weight or with a flower press.
Pressing with an iron.
Standing in water.
Placing in a high temperature.

Using desiccants (substances which withdraw moisture).
Secondly, absorption of glycerine.

DRYING

Drying gives long-lasting results (sometimes for years) in plants with strong tissue, but those with weak tissue may be very fragile to handle.

When a plant reaches the end of its growth cycle the rate of transpiration (the evaporation of moisture from the plant surfaces) exceeds that of water absorption, with the result that the plant shrivels and dies. If it is to be used in an arrangement, the shrivelling, which is unattractive, must somehow be prevented or kept to a minimum. The following methods are aimed at keeping the shape of plants when they become dehydrated.

Hanging up to Dry

Plants respond differently as they dry out and those with strong, rigid tissue often keep their shape even when completely dry. Evidence of this can be seen in the herbaceous border in the cold months. If, in addition, the evaporation of water is gradual, the shape is kept especially well.

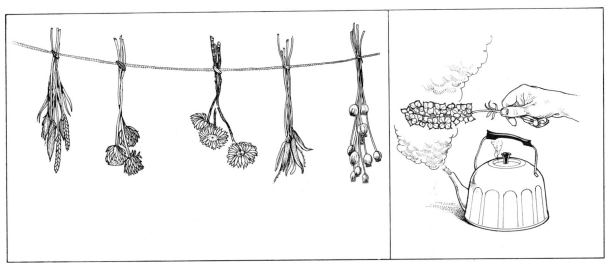

Plant material hanging up to dry. Crushed material can be restored by steaming

Left: Glycerined, dried and fresh plant materials can be arranged together with great success

Right: A spray of orchids makes a striking design with two tree roots and glycerined aspidistra leaves

An arrangement of dried plant material

Some plants, then, dry naturally and well out of doors, keeping their shape, but they may suffer damage from weather conditions and better results are obtained from indoor drying in a dry room. Hanging up to dry is a method to be used only for plants with strong rigid tissue which easily keep their shape.

METHOD
1. Remove the leaves, as these do not dry well.
2. Tie the stems into small bunches with the flowers at different lengths, so that they do not crush each other.
3. Hang upside down, to help the preservation of the shape and to avoid drooping stems, in a warm place with a free circulation of air.

The plant material is ready for use when it feels quite dry. The time varies according to the type of plant material.

Store. When free of moisture the plant material can be stored in a dry room. It may be put in boxes with tissue paper to minimise crushing, placed upright in jars of sand or hung up. Mildewing and loss of rigidity occur if the dried plant material is stored in a damp atmosphere.

Restore. Steaming can restore shape lost by crushing. Hold the plant material over the spout of a boiling kettle for a few seconds and then quickly reshape with the fingers and if necessary stuff any cavities with tissue paper.

Colour. There is always a certain amount of dulling although drying in a dark place prevents some loss of colour. It is advisable to keep the dried plant material out of strong light at all times. Dipping the flower heads in alum or borax, before hanging up to dry, also prevents colour fading. The powder should be shaken off before use.

Suitable Plant Material

Acanthus (Bear's Breeches). Perennial. White and purple summer flowers.
Achillea (Yarrow). Perennial. White or yellow flowers then seed heads.
Acroclinium. Annual. Pink and white summer flowers.
Agapanthus (African Lily). Perennial. Seed heads.
Allium (Ornamental Onion). Bulb. White, yellow, purple or blue globular flowers in spring and summer then seed heads.
Amaranthus caudatus (Love-lies-bleeding). Annual. Crimson or lime-green tassel flowers in summer.
Anaphalis (Pearly Everlasting). Perennial. Small

silvery flowers carried in clusters in summer.
Angelica (Holy Ghost). Perennial. Seed heads.
Anthriscus sylvestris. (Cow Parsley). Biennial. Fruits.
Artemisia absinthium (Wormwood). Perennial. Yellow summer flowers.
Briza maxima (Quaking Grass). Annual. Seed heads.
Bromus (Ornamental Oats). Annual. Seed heads.
Calluna (Ling). Evergreen shrub. Late summer flowers in a range of colours.
Celosia (Cockscomb). Annual. Summer flowers in shades of pink, yellow, red and white.
Clematis. Evergreen and deciduous climbers. Seed heads.
Coix lachryma-jobi (Job's Tears). Annual grass. Seed heads.
Cortaderia (Pampas Grass). Perennial. Silken flower plumes.
Cynara cardunculus (Cardoon). Perennial. Purple summer flowers.
Delphinium. Annual and perennial. Summer flowers in shades of blue, purple, red and white.
Dipsacus fullonum (Teasel). Biennial. Seed head.
Echinops (Globe Thistle). Perennial. Blue or white summer flowers.
Erica (Heather). Evergreen shrub. White to crimson flowers produced all year on various varieties and species.
Eryngium (Sea Holly). Perennial. Blue, purple or white summer flowers.
Helichrysum (Everlasting, Straw Flowers). Annual. Summer flowers in many bright colours.
Helipterum (Rhodanthe). Annual. Pink or white summer flowers.
Hemerocallis (Day Lily). Perennial. Fruits.
Heracleum sphondylium (Hogweed). Biennial. Seed heads.
Hordeum jubatum (Squirrel's Tail Grass). Perennial. Seed heads.

Iris. Perennials or bulbs. Capsules and seeds.
Lagurus ovatus (Hare's Tail Grass). Annual. Seed heads.
Lavender. Evergreen shrub. Summer flowers in lavender, purple or white.
Limonium (Sea Lavender, Statice). Annual and perennial. Late summer flowers in blue, pink, white and yellow.
Lunaria annua (Honesty). Biennial. Seed heads.
Molucella laevis (Bells of Ireland). Annual. Green and white flowers in summer.
Nicandra physaloides (Shoo-fly Plant). Annual. Fruits.
Nigella damascena (Love-in-a-mist). Annual. Fruits.
Panicum violaceum (Foxtail Millet). Annual. Seed heads.
Papaver orientalis (Oriental Poppy). Perennial. Seed heads.
Physalis franchetii (Chinese Lantern). Perennial. Fruits.
Protea. Tender evergreen shrub. Spring flowers.
Rumex (Dock). Perennial. Seed heads.
Rushes, Sedges, Cereals. Perennials and annuals. Seed heads.
Salix (Pussy Willow). Tree. Catkins.
Tricholaena rosea. Perennial grass. Seed heads.
Triticum (Ornamental Wheat). Annual. Seed heads.
Typha (Reedmace usually called Bulrush). Perennial. Seed heads.
Verbascum (Mullein). Biennial. Fruits.

Pressing under a Weight or with a Flower Press

A flower press can be bought or made and this gives excellent results. Alternatively plant material can be put under a heavy weight. Pressing stops shrivelling but flattens the material. Hanging plant material to dry, as previously

A flower press can be easily constructed and makes the plant material paper-thin

Plant material arranged for pressing on a sheet of blotting paper. Some flowers press better dismantled

described, helps to keep the three-dimensional shape but this method is not suitable for plants with fine tissue for which pressing is best. Pressing reduces the water content successfully but at the expense of the three-dimensional shape. It is not a suitable method for plant material with rigid tissue such as achillea (yarrow) or for fleshy succulent plants with a high moisture content. Flowers which have a heavy hard centre are not suitable either because the petals cannot be pressed firmly down. The flat thin type of plant material is the most successful.

Pressed leaves and grasses can be used in arrangements in containers, although their appearance can be rather flat. The most important use of pressed plant material is for flower pictures which make very lovely, permanent decorations for the home. Small flowers and leaves are the most useful for this purpose.

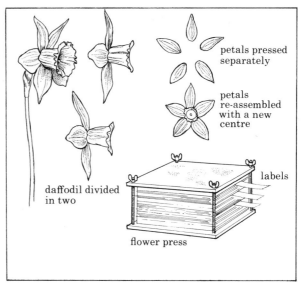

Method of arranging plant material for pressing

MAKING A FLOWER PRESS. Collect:
(A) 2 pieces of 5-ply wood, each 12 in. square.
(B) 4 5-in. bolts with wing nuts.
(C) Heavy cardboard.
(D) Blotting paper.

Make holes for the bolts, one in each corner of both pieces of wood. Cut 11 pieces of cardboard each 12 in. square and cut off all the corners. Put 2 pieces (20 in all) of blotting paper between each piece of cardboard, beginning and ending with cardboard.

METHOD OF PRESSING
1. Pick the plant material on a dry day but not until after mid-day to give the dew a chance to dry out.
2. Cut off all the stem from each piece.
3. Arrange carefully on a sheet of blotting paper and make sure that the flowers and leaves do not touch each other. If the centre of the flower is hard, press it down firmly with the thumb. Flowers that are especially three dimensional or have hard centres are better dismantled. The petals can then be re-assembled for the pressed flower picture and given another centre. Stems may be sellotaped into curves.

Three-dimensional flowers, such as daffodils, should be dissected into two with scissors and then pressed. Each daffodil will give two 'flowers' for a picture. The trumpet and the perianth segments which back it may also be separated for pressing. After the plant material has been carefully arranged, roll a piece of blotting paper over it.
4. Press under heavy books, a carpet, bricks or in a flower press. The plant material should be left undisturbed for at least six weeks in a warm room.

It may be necessary, however, to change the blotting paper if the plant material was rather fleshy in the first place, as the paper can become damp and mouldy. If a press is used, tighten the wing nuts regularly.

Plant material intended for flower pictures should be pressed for at least three months and if possible for a year. The longer it is left the more paper thin it becomes and the colours do not fade as readily when exposed to light.
5. If possible, label each pressing with the contents and the date when pressing began, to avoid disturbance. The label can stick out of the book used for pressing, or a sticky label can be placed on the outside of the blotting paper.

Store. In a very dry place in boxes. Place tissue paper between the specimens.
Restore. The less fragile flowers and leaves can be restored by placing them between tissue paper and ironing them gently with a slightly warm iron. A steam iron may also be used over blotting paper. Coarse leaves may be dipped in salad oil, placed between sheets of newspaper and pressed with a hot steam iron.
Colour. Colours change and fade during pressing. They are none the less beautiful for the result is often soft, muted colours with cream, yellow, brown, beige and grey predominating. It is fascinating to see how various leaves and flowers respond to pressing. Young maple becomes pale green or yellow, young ash turns black, most roses become cream but a deep red one turns brown. Grey leaves often remain grey. Yellow and orange fade least and blue remains in a delphinium but other blues fade more quickly. The best flower for keeping its colour is the yellow anthemis daisy.

A Christmas arrangement of chrysanthemums, copper-painted dried seed pods and roots with plastic leaves in an antique Chinese bronze container. Only one flower is seen full face because of their large size

Suitable Plant Material

Acer (Maple). Tree. Very ornamental foliage in a range of colours.

Adiantum (Maidenhair Fern). Fronds of elegant leaves.

Ampelosis (Vine). Climber. Attractive lobed leaves.

Anthemis (Chamomile). Perennial. Both the summer flowers and the stalks are suitable for pressing.

Astrantia (Hattie's Pincushion). Perennial. Pink and white flowers and flower centres.

Auricula. Perennial. Spring flowers in many colours.

Bellis perennis (Lawn Daisy). Perennial. White flowers.

Calendula (Pot Marigold). Annual. Flower centres.

Castanea (Sweet Chestnut). Tree. Long, pointed leaves.

Cineraria maritima. Annual. Grey foliage.

Clematis. Evergreen and deciduous climbers. Flowers in all colours.

Clematis montana. Foliage and stalks.

Coreopsis (Tickseed). Perennial. Yellow and crimson summer flowers.

Cornus (Dogwood). Trees and shrubs. White, pink or yellow flowers in spring and summer.

Cosmos (Cosmea). Annual. Pink, crimson, white or yellow flowers in summer.

Crocosmia. Corm. Ribbed, sword-shaped leaves.

Cytisus (Broom). Shrub. White, pink, crimson or yellow flowers in spring or summer.

Delphinium. Annual and perennial. Summer flowers in shades of blue, pink and white.

Eschscholzia (Californian Poppy). Annual. Yellow, red, pink or white flowers in summer.

Fagus. (Beech). Tree. Green or purple foliage.

Ferns. All kinds. Mostly rather feathery foliage.

Fraxinus (Ash). Tree. Compound leaves made up of sprays of leaflets.

Geranium robertianum (Herb Robert). Annual. Deeply indented foliage.

Gladiolus. Corm. Broad, sword-shaped foliage.

Grasses. All kinds. Foliage.

Hedera (Ivy). Evergreen climber. Foliage in a range of shapes, sizes and variegations.

Heuchera sanguinea (Coral Bells). Perennial. Red flowers in summer.

Hydrangea. Shrubs and climbers. Flower heads separated. White, pink, blue to purple.

Iris. Perennial and bulb. Broad, sword-shaped foliage.

Laburnum. Tree. Yellow trails of flowers in spring and early summer.

Lonicera (Honeysuckle). Deciduous and ever-green climbers and shrubs. A variety of foliage.

Montbretia. Corm. Sword-shaped foliage and yellow or orange flowers in summer.

Narcissus family. Bulbs. Flowers dismantled before pressing.

Nicotiana (Tobacco Plant). Annual. White, green or pink flowers in summer.

Papaver (Poppies). Annual and perennial. Flower centres of all the types.

Papaver nudicaule (Iceland Poppy). Annual. Summer flowers in yellow, orange, pink and white.

Parthenocissus (Virginia Creeper). Climber. Lobed foliage, good autumn colour.

Pelargonium (Zonal Geranium). Perennial. Elaborately variegated foliage.

Polyanthus. Perennial. Spring flowers in many colours.

Populus tremula (Aspen). Tree. Dark green foliage.

Primula (Primrose). Perennial. Flowers and stalks.

Prunus (Cherry, Plum, Peach). Tree. Tapering oval foliage.

Quercus (Oak). Tree. Oval leaves with deep rounded lobes.

Ranunculus (Buttercup). Perennial. Yellow summer flowers and stalks.

Ranunculus ficaria (Celandine). Perennial. Yellow flowers.

Rhus (Sumach). Tree. Long leaves made up of leaflets, good autumn colour.

Rose. Shrub. Flower petals.

Rubus (Blackberry). Shrub. Foliage.

Senecio. Shrubs and perennials. Many with grey foliage.

Sorbus aria (Whitebeam). Tree. Foliage covered in white silky down.

Trifolium (Clover, Trefoil). Perennial. Flowers and stalks.

Venidio-arctotis. Annual. Flowers in pink, orange, copper and red.

Vicia (Vetch). Perennial. Flowers.

Viola (Violet, Pansy). Perennials. Flowers over a long period in many colours.

Pressing with an Iron

A few varieties of plant material can be dried rapidly with an iron but the results do not last as long as slow pressing.

METHOD

1. Place the plant material between blotting paper or newspaper.
2. Press with the iron at 'Wool' setting for about five minutes depending on the thickness of the

plant material. Lift off the top piece of paper now and again during pressing to release the steam. At first the leaf will become very limp but it stiffens again during ironing.
3. Place under a weight in the airing cupboard overnight.

Store. In a dry place in a box.
Colour. This is usually brown or dull green.

Suitable Plant Material

Acer (Maple). Tree. Very decorative foliage.
Aesculus (Horse Chestnut). Tree. Ornamental leaves composed of a number of leaflets.
Codiaeum (Croton). House plant. Broad sword-shaped leaves in a range of bright colours.
Crocosmia and Montbretia. Corms. Ribbed, sword-shaped leaves.
Fagus (Beech). Tree. Green or purple foliage.
Gladiolus. Corm. Sword-shaped leaves.
Grasses. All kinds. Foliage.
Rhus (Sumach). Tree. Long leaves made up of leaflets.
Rushes and Sedges. Perennials with long thin leaves.

Codiaeum, oak and maple leaves can be treated in another way by dipping them in melted candle wax and then ironing them between sheets of newspaper.

Standing in Water

Plants with exceptionally strong stems respond to gradual drying while the stem end is in water.

METHOD
1. Pick when the flower is beginning to dry on the plant in the garden.
2. Stand in half an inch of water in a jar.
3. Do not top up the water if it is absorbed by the plant material.

Store. In a dry place, in boxes, standing up in a jar of sand or hanging up.
Restore. Steaming is an effective method.
Colour. There is some fading, but hydrangeas may keep their colour.

Suitable Plant Material

Achillea (Yarrow). Perennial. White or yellow summer flowers.
Calluna (Ling). Evergreen shrub. Late summer flowers in many colours.
Erica (Heather). Evergreen shrub. White to crimson flowers.

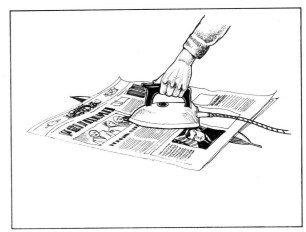
Pressing with an iron

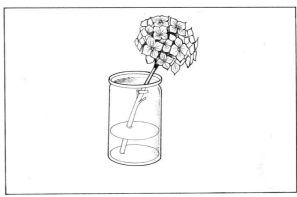
Drying a hydrangea by standing it in water

Hydrangea. Shrubs and climbers. Flowers in white, pink, blue to purple.

High Temperature Drying

Single fruits dry well if placed in a hot airing cupboard until light in weight, which means that the water has evaporated.

METHOD
1. Wipe the fruit over with a mild disinfectant to discourage mildew.
2. Place the fruit in a dark corner of the airing cupboard and remove when dry and light.

Gourds will last indefinitely but, because of the thick outer covering, can take as long as three months to dry out. They turn a lovely beige in colour.

Artichokes, bought from the greengrocer, will often open out into mauve flowers in a few days. When quite light in weight they should be taken out of the airing cupboard. The mauve flower eventually turns beige.

Store. In a dry place.
Colour. Little of the original colouring is left but the mellow tones are pleasing.

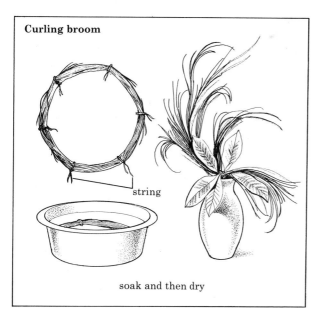

Curling broom

string

soak and then dry

Suitable Plant Material

Acorns
Artichokes
Avocado pears
Capsicums
Gourds
Pomegranates
Rose hips
Small oranges. These may be studded with cloves, which are preservatives, to make sweet-smelling pomanders for wardrobes. The pomander is more decorative if rows of straw flowers alternate with the cloves to cover all the fruit.
Broom. This is especially successful dried this way – tie pieces of it into circles and soak for two hours in water. Dry, still tied, in the airing cupboard for a further two days, then untie into swirling permanent curves. These may be painted with spray paint for exciting effects.

Using Desiccants

Certain substances withdraw and retain the water from plants. They are silica gel, borax, alum and sand, which has been used for drying plants for many centuries.

If care is taken, plant material dried with desiccants can last for many years but it is often very fragile and as the flowers must be handled carefully this is a method for those with patience.

Through experience, flower arrangers develop a preference for one or other of the desiccants. The time for leaving the plant material in each type varies considerably.
Silica gel. This is popular because it is quick acting, 48 to 72 hours, and the shortened time

helps to retain the colour well in the plant material. It is heavier than the other desiccants and suitable for stronger tissues. About 5 lb. is sufficient for normal use. It is very granular and absorbs 50 per cent. of its own weight in moisture. It can sometimes be bought ground more finely, which is ideal, or it can be crushed with a rolling pin. After use it will not dry plant material again if it contains a lot of water. An indicator is sold with silica gel and this turns blue when the substance is ready for use, but is pink otherwise. Place the gel in an oven at a temperature of 250°F. to dry it. Remove when the indicator turns blue when it is plunged into the centre. The silica gel should not be handled for some time after being in the oven as it retains the heat.
Borax and/or Alum. Drying fine, delicate plant material requires the use of the lightest of the desiccants – borax or alum. The length of time taken to dry the flowers depends on the coarseness of the tissue and the warmth of the surroundings and is from one to six weeks. Both substances can each be used separately or they may be mixed together (half of each). Borax tends to be adhesive and difficult to remove from the petals of flowers and it also gives less support than silica gel. Borax is heavier if mixed with sand (two parts of borax to one of sand) and this mixture gives better support, which is necessary while drying is taking place to hold the petals in position. Borax and alum do not penetrate cavities easily and care should be taken to see that the powder covers all parts of each petal. Dry the powders after use in an airing cupboard.
Sand. This flows well and penetrates cavities easily. The results have a good texture and keep a natural gloss. The flowers may be left indefinitely in the sand without harm. It is also heavy enough to support flower petals well but is rather too heavy for delicate flowers. However, it can be modified by adding 3 parts of borax to heavy sand and 1 part of borax to light sand. Better colours result from mixing 1 tablespoonful of bicarbonate of soda with 15 lb. of sand. (A 1-lb. coffee tin holds 4 lb. of sand.)

Sand needs cleaning before use – fill a bucket three-quarters full of it, add water to the top and remove any floating debris. Pour off the water and fill again with more water to which 1 teaspoonful of detergent has been added. Stir, pour off the water and rinse by turning the sand over several times in clear water. Dry in an oven, temperature 250°F., for 4 to 5 hours, or in the sun for 2 to 3 hours. Sift before use.

Sand only needs one cleaning but it will be necessary to dry it after each use.

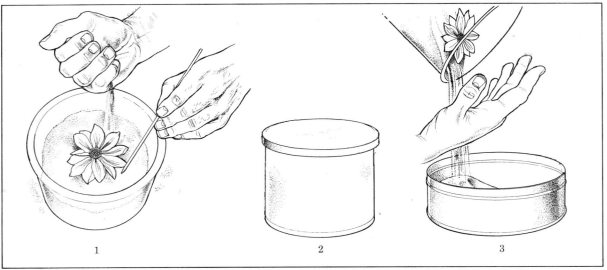

Preservation with desiccants 1. Pour on the desiccant using a stick to dress the flower 2. Cover the flower completely with desiccant and replace the lid 3. Pour off the desiccant in a steady stream

METHOD OF USING DESICCANTS

The plant material is buried in the drying substance and left undisturbed until the moisture has been withdrawn. The time varies according to the plant material, the warmth of the room and the type of desiccant.

1. Pick the plant material on a dry day, after noon. Pick only specimens which are in the peak of condition and undamaged. Plant material that is not full blown is more successful.

2. Cut the stems about $\frac{1}{2}$ to 1 in. long.

3. Pour about 1 in. of the desiccant into a tin and level it. A $\frac{1}{2}$-lb. coffee tin with a plastic lid takes one medium-sized flower.

4. Place the flower on top with the stem in the desiccant.

5. Cover the flower gently with more desiccant, lifting each petal to make sure that the powder goes into all the cavities. This gives even drying and better support to keep the shape. It is helpful to 'dress' the flower with a pointed stick such as a toothpick. Continue covering gently until there is a depth of about 1 in. of the desiccant over all the flower.

6. Place a lid on the box and keep it in a warm place. If more than one flower is put in the tin, they should not touch each other, and should be of the same variety or need similar timing. They should feel crisp like taffeta when dry.

7. Remove the flower, when you expect it to be ready, by gently pouring off the desiccant in a steady stream without reversing the motion. The flower eventually drops into the hand. Dust away loose particles with a soft brush. Glue on any loose petals.

Store. In a tin containing a few grains of desiccant to prevent the flower taking up moisture again. Keep in a dry place.

Colours. These are often extremely good but the plant material should be kept away from strong light to prevent fading. The stability of colour depends on the original colour and the flower. Reds and violets are quite stable but become darker. Greens, yellows and oranges fade more quickly. Dark colours do not fade as quickly as light colours. Salt added to borax and sand helps to stabilise colours.

Restore. Petals which fall off can be replaced by glueing with a tiny spot of clear glue. Dull petals may be stroked with a little oil which will give a greater sheen. Clean with dry cleaning fluid.

Faults

(A) Stiff, crisp petals indicate that the drying has been too rapid.

(B) A wrinkled appearance is caused by insufficient weight on the petals – try a heavier desiccant.

(C) Damp spots mean that the desiccant was not evenly distributed.

Records. When drying it is helpful to keep records of the type of flower, desiccant and time.

Suitable Plant Material

The numbers in the following list indicate the approximate number of weeks for drying in *sand*. *Borax* and *alum* take half the time. *Silica gel* takes from 48 to 72 hours according to the strength of the petals.

Althaea (Hollyhock). Perennial, biennial and annual. Spikes of summer flowers in many colours. Use flowers singly. [2]

Anemone. Perennial. Many types, so flowers occur throughout the year. [2]

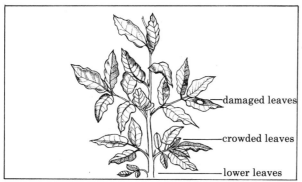

Remove all damaged, crowded and lower leaves before glycerining

Azalea. Deciduous and evergreen shrubs with flowers in many lovely colours. [2]
Calendula (Marigold). Annual. Yellow or orange summer flowers. [2]
Camellia. Evergreen shrub. White to crimson flowers in winter and spring. [2]
Clematis. Evergreen and deciduous climbers. Flowers are in all colours and are better dried face down. [3]
Cosmos (Cosmea). Annual. Summer flowers dried face down. [2]
Dahlia. Perennial. Summer flowers in most colours. [2]
Dianthus (Carnation). Perennial. Flowers mainly in white to crimson range. [2]
Foliage. All kinds. [2]
Gerbera (Transvaal Daisy). Tender perennial. Yellow, red, pink and orange summer flowers. [2]
Hellebore (Christmas and Lenten Rose). Peren-

A gradual change of colour is seen as the glycerine mixture creeps up the leaf

nials. White to maroon or green winter and spring flowers. [2]
Nymphaea (Water Lily). White, yellow, pink to crimson summer flowers. [2]
Orchid. Many types and colours. [4]
Peony. Perennials and shrubs. Early summer flowers in shades of yellow, pink and red, also in white. [2]
Primula (Primrose). Perennial. Spring flowers in many colours. [2]
Rose. Shrubs and climbers. Flowers in all colours. [2]
Syringa (Lilac). Shrub. White, maroon, mauve and purple summer flowers. [2]
Viburnum opulus sterile (Snowball Tree). White flowers in early summer. [2]
Viola (Violet and Pansy). Perennials. Richly coloured flowers over a long period. [2]
Zinnia. Annual. Brightly coloured summer flowers. [2]

ABSORPTION OF GLYCERINE

Preservation by absorption of glycerine is a very popular and easy method. The results are supple and not brittle as with the drying method and shrivelling of the shape is prevented by the presence of the glycerine. The natural colours are not retained as with drying. Many varieties of plant material become very tough after absorbing glycerine and some can be almost indestructible.

When a plant begins to dry, it stops absorbing moisture from the ground and at this stage it will not absorb glycerine either. Therefore, treatment must be given during the growing period. The glycerine is taken up through the end of the stem and gradually reaches every part of the cutting to give perfect preservation. Because glycerine is more viscous (like treacle) than water, it must be mixed with water so that it can be taken up by the plant. Eventually the water in the mixture evaporates from the plant leaving the glycerine behind in the plant cells. This method of preservation is the most suitable for leaves, although a few flowers and seed heads respond well. Experiments may be made with adding dyes to glycerine to alter the colouring.

METHOD
1. Pour into a jar 1 measure of glycerine and 2 similar measures of hot water and stir well.
2. Cut plant material which is in good condition. The most suitable time for the majority of plants is when they are at their best – mature, but not old and beginning to dry. Young foliage does not

Mopping an aspidistra leaf before placing the stem end in the glycerine mixture

Some smaller leaves such as ivy can be preserved by submerging them in the mixture of glycerine and water

take up any moisture readily and will usually flop if placed in the glycerine mixture. July is a good month in the British Isles for many plants. Any length of stem may be treated including beech branches of about 6 ft. To avoid waste remove any damaged and unwanted leaves before standing the stems in glycerine.

3. Place the stem ends in the glycerine and water mixture, which should cover about two inches of the end of the stem. The stem ends should have been previously treated as for conditioning (page 16). It does no harm to place the stem ends in the mixture while it is hot – and it is helpful for rapid absorption.

4. More of the mixture should be added to the jar if the original amount is used up. There is no waste as it can be used over and over again.

5. Remove the plant material when it has changed colour. As a general rule the tougher the leaf, the longer the time necessary. Many leaves show the glycerine creeping along the tissues, for example, a laurel leaf will appear green where the glycerine has not reached it and brown in the other parts. It is easy to leave thin beech leaves too long in the mixture and then beads of glycerine appear on the leaf surfaces. The beads should be wiped off with cotton wool otherwise greasy marks may be left on wallpaper when the beech is placed in an arrangement.

Mould sometimes occurs in the glycerine mixture if it is kept for a while. This may be avoided if $\frac{1}{4}$ teaspoonful of chlorhexidine (or any mild disinfectant) is added to 1 pint of the mixture before use.

Store. Preserved plant material can be stored in boxes in a dry place. Mildewing occurs if there is any dampness present and this is difficult to remove. As the results of preservation with glycerine are supple and tough there is no need for careful packing with tissue paper. Glycerined plant material may be washed in water containing detergent. Dry thoroughly.

Colour. The natural colour of the plant material is not retained and the resulting colours are usually in many variations of browns, dark greens, blue-grey and purple-grey. It is possible to lighten the colours by placing them in strong sunshine *after* preservation. This works especially well with beech leaves. Remove from the sun when the desired colour is reached.

Mopping Foliage

Some plants, especially those with heavy tissue such as aspidistra, absorb moisture of any kind slowly and as a result the tips may dry out before the glycerine reaches them. This gives a half-brittle, half-supple result which is not satisfactory. To minimise this drying, mop the outside of the leaf, on both sides, with the glycerine mixture *before* standing the stem end in it. Cotton wool may be used for mopping. Aspidistra, *Fatsia japonica*, large ivy, anthurium, dracaena, fatshedera and *Ficus elastica* leaves should always be mopped.

Immersion

Smaller leaves, which absorb moisture slowly, may be submerged in the glycerine mixture in a shallow pie dish. This suits small ivy, violet, galax, lily of the valley, *Fatsia japonica*, hosta, fig, bergenia and fern leaves and other foliage which may prove difficult to glycerine otherwise.

Suitable Plant Materials

The numbers in the following list indicate the approximate length of time in weeks required for preservation. Unless otherwise stated, treat in mid-summer in Britain.

Acer pseudoplatanus (Sycamore). Tree. Winged fruits. [2]

Adiantum (Maidenhair Fern). Dainty sprays of

small leaflets on wiry stems. Any time. [2 to 3]

Anthurium. House plant. Large heart-shaped leaves. Any time. [3 to 4]

Aspidistra. House plant. Green or variegated leaves. Any time. [12]

Aucuba. Evergreen shrub. Shiny green or spotted foliage. [3 to 4]

Bergenia. Perennial. Roundish glossy leaves. [3 to 4]

Buxus (Box). Evergreen shrub. Small dark green leaves. [3 to 4]

Camellia. Evergreen shrub. Shiny leaves. [4]

Castanea (Sweet Chestnut). Tree. Long pointed leaves. The prickly cases containing the chestnuts are also useful. [3]

Choisya ternata (Mexican Orange Blossom). Evergreen shrub. Dark green shiny leaves. [4 to 5]

Clematis vitalba (Old Man's Beard). Climber. Shoots picked before the flowers open. [2]

Cotoneaster. Evergreen and deciduous shrubs. Time varies with variety. [2 to 3]

Dipsacus fullonum (Teasel). Perennial. Seed heads. [3]

Dracaena. House plant. Handsome, often variegated foliage. [12]

Elaeagnus pungens. Evergreen and deciduous shrubs. Green and variegated foliage. [4 to 6]

Eryngium (Sea Holly). Perennial. Unusual flowers surrounded by spiny bracts. [2 to 3]

Eucalyptus. Tree. Greyish-green foliage. [2 to 3]

Fagus (Beech). Tree. Foliage. [1]

Fatshedera. House plant. Ivy-like leaves. [4 to 6]

Fatsia japonica. House plant. Green and variegated multi-lobed leaves. [2 to 10]

Ferns. All kinds. Pick fronds when spores are visible on the backs. [2 to 3]

Ficus elastica (Rubber Plant). House plant. Leathery green or variegated leaves. [4]

Grevillea robusta. House plant. Feathery foliage. Any time. [2]

Hedera (Ivy). Evergreen climber. Green and variegated foliage. [3]

Helleborus corsicus (Corsican Hellebore). Perennial. Deeply divided leaves. [3]

Hydrangea. Shrubs and climbers. Flower heads, a woody stem is needed. [2]

Iris. Bulbs and perennials. Fruits. [2]

Laurus nobilis (Laurel). Evergreen shrub. Dark green oval leaves. [4]

Liriodendron tulipifera (Tulip Tree). Leaves of unusual shape. [2 to 3]

Magnolia grandiflora. Tree. Evergreen leaves. [3 to 4]

Mahonia. Evergreen shrub. Holly-like leaves. [3 to 6]

Molucella laevis (Bells of Ireland). Annual.

Unusual green bracts around the flowers. [3]

Peony. Shrubs and perennials. Divided green leaves. [2]

Pittosporum tenuifolium. Shrub. Leaves with wavy margins and black stems. [2]

Polygonatum odoratum (Solomon's Seal). Perennial. Long green leaves picked after the plants have flowered. [1]

Quercus (Oak). Tree. Lobed leaves. [2]

Rose. Sprays of green leaves, a woody stem is needed. [2]

Sorbus aria (Whitebeam). Tree. Green, white or grey leaves. [1½]

Other plant material should be experimented with and this is easy if a jar of glycerine and water is kept constantly available. There is no waste if the plant material fails to take up any glycerine.

MECHANICS FOR PRESERVED PLANT MATERIAL

Dried Plant Material

The stems may be supported in dry plastic foam, Plasticine, a pinholder or more permanently in plaster of Paris or slow-drying cement. If dried and fresh plant material (which needs water) are to be combined in an arrangement regularly or for any length of time, it is necessary to dip the stem ends of the dried plant material in melted candle wax, sealing wax or nail polish for protection against the water. If the stem is cut, it should be re-dipped. Dried flowers without stems may be glued to branches or twigs or they may be wired. (See below.)

Glycerined Plant Material

The stem ends may be supported by the same methods as fresh plant material. Sometimes mildewing can occur and if it does cut off the mildewed parts of the stem and then seal the stem end as described in the previous paragraph.

Wiring

Single leaves and cones may be wired as described on page 11.

Dried flowers may be wired by pushing a stub wire through the centre of the flower. Turn over a small hook at the end and pull this down into the centre of the flower. The stub wire may be bound with florist's tape. Alternatively, the stub wire may be placed into a hollow dried stem, saved for this purpose. The stems of dried flowers

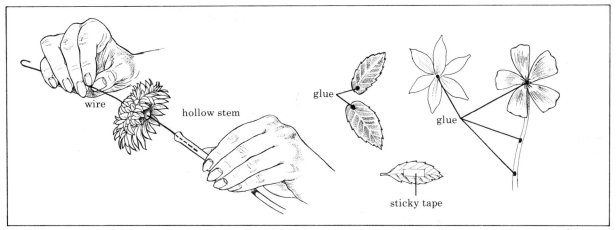

Left: Wiring a dried flower with a stub wire. *Right:* Sticky tape or a glue such as Copydex can be used to fix plant material to the background

are seldom usable, with the exception of achillea and hydrangea, as they become too brittle.

PRESSED FLOWER PICTURES

The design may be arranged on heavy paper, mounting board or fabric-covered board. A flat thin knife is useful for lifting the fragile plant material and placing it in position. It is wise to complete the design before sticking and to use small flowers and leaves. It is best to do this in a draught-free room and to cover the design with a board or glass whenever it is left before sticking. This prevents pieces floating out of place.

The best method of fixing the plant material to the background is with small spots of Copydex, or a latex type adhesive. This does not show through the pressed flowers and leaves even after years, as do the other types of glue. Another advantage of Copydex is that it can be removed easily without leaving marks. It is not necessary to cover the back of the flower or leaf completely with adhesive and small spots are sufficient to hold the plant material in position.

Mounting

The paper backing should be placed on hardboard and covered with glass which is pressed well down on to the plant material. The glass may be held in place by a frame or clips. No mount should be used as this prevents the glass from pressing down on to the plant material. A backing board is needed to obtain adequate pressure. It is a good idea to buy an old frame from a market stall and remove the backing. Cover this with paper or fabric, stick the design on and then replace the frame.

Binding a stub-wire stem with florists' tape

When making a pressed flower picture it is important that the glass is pressed down on to the plant material

PLAQUES

These use three-dimensional plant material mounted on to a background which is visible. It may be of any shape and can be either framed or unframed. There are several methods of making plaques.

Background

This may be made of hardboard, wood or pegboard cut to any shape.

Finishes

Suggestions:
(A) Fabric, mitred at the corners with the edges glued to the back of the plaque. Raw edges may be neatened by covering with sticky tape or paper.
(B) Fablon stuck to the board and turned over for a few inches on to the back.
(C) Cork sheeting glued to the board.
(D) Stain which is suitable for wood and is very attractive when the wood is well sanded. Varnish or polish may be used on top of the stain.

(E) Reed matting glued to the board.
(F) Paint, the most attractive is usually emulsion.
(G) Plaster of Paris or self-hardening clay applied roughly to the surface of the board and then painted.

Mechanics

There are several methods:
1. Squeeze quick-drying clear glue on to the back of each piece of plant material. Uhu or a similar PVA adhesive is good.
2. Make a mound of slow-drying cement on the background. This takes about half an hour to set giving time to push the ends of the plant material into the cement. Stems can easily be removed and replaced during this time.
3. Wire each piece of plant material and push it through the holes in the pegboard (and any fabric covering it). Twist the wires around each other at the back and cut off spare wire, flattening the ends against the back of the board. Further plant material can also be glued on to the front.
4. Cover a block of dried plastic foam with $\frac{1}{2}$-in. mesh wire netting. Run short pieces from a reel of wire through the netting and twist them around a few nails knocked into the front of the board. Push stems of the plant material into the foam through the netting.

Hanging. Two ring screws and a cord may be attached to the back of the plaque so that it can be hung on a wall.

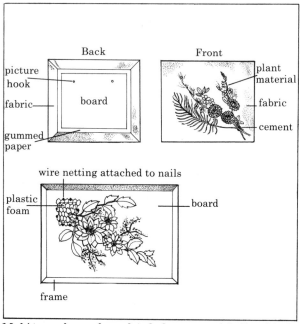

Making a plaque from dried plant material. Two kinds of mechanics are shown, cement and plastic foam

SWAGS

In a swag the design of the plant material roughly follows the shape of the background, which is not visible in the finished article. The background may be made of hardboard, wood or pegboard. It should be cut smaller than desired for the finished swag as the plant material will overlap the edges. No covering need be put on the background as it is not visible. The mechanics are the same as for plaques. Highlights of gold or copper may be lightly sprayed on to the dried plant material in a plaque or swag, using paint in an aerosol can.

Plaques and swags can also be made with fresh plant material and instructions for these are given on pages 117 and 118

GLITTERING DRIED MATERIAL

This can be attractive for Christmas decorations, and there are several methods and colours.
1. Apply glitter spray from an aerosol can.
2. Pour the glitter into a saucer. Using a brush, paint clear glue or varnish on to the parts of the plant material to be glittered. When it has dried a little and is tacky, dip the glued surfaces into the glitter. Shake off any excess.
3. The plant material may be completely sprayed with paint or varnish from an aerosol can. Pour glitter over this at once. To save wasting glitter do this over a sheet of newspaper.

A plaque of silver birch bark and sliced hogweed stems. It may be framed

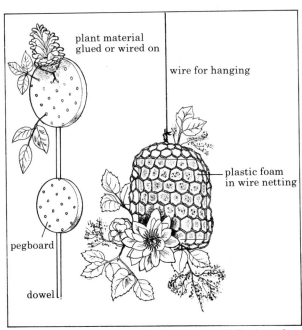

Making a swag from dried plant material. Pegboard or plastic foam and wire netting are used for the base

A swag of preserved and dried plant material in shades of pink, orange and brown constructed on pegboard

Driftwood

As you progress in flower arrangement it is exciting to realise that it has become a really broad subject in recent years. It is no longer a matter only of placing flowers in containers of water and neither are flowers and leaves the only kind of plant material that can be assembled into interesting and beautiful designs. Our Victorian ancestors would not have dreamt of using wood tossed up from the sea to decorate their homes but recent generations have discovered that weathered wood has great beauty.

The name given by flower arrangers to weathered wood of all descriptions is 'driftwood'. This term refers to roots, crosscuts of trunks, barks, tree stumps, leafless branches, woody stems such as ivy and large chunks, all of which have been weathered by the elements and not necessarily tossed up from the sea. Driftwood is as much plant material as leaves, berries and flowers. It can be combined with other plant material as part of the design, placed to hide mechanics, used as a base or made into a container. It may also be used alone, looking rather like a piece of modern sculpture, and is often as beautiful.

No two pieces of driftwood ever look exactly the same and their ageless and unique qualities are especially fascinating. When properly treated driftwood will also fit into any home and little can match the pride of finding and preparing one's own pieces to use for decoration.

Finding Wood

Florists sometimes sell driftwood as it is not always possible for city-dwellers to get into the country to look for it. For those that have easy access to the countryside, no walk can ever be dull when it is realised that round any corner could be hiding an interesting piece of wood. The best places to look are lakesides, seashores, woodland, bonfires and mountainsides. Wherever trees grow there will be odd pieces of wood for the finding. One might expect summer to be the best time to look but storms are less frequent and bracken can hide the pieces. Early spring, after winter storms and before there is much under-growth, is a very good time. It is wise to ask permission to take wood away if it is on private ground.

Never take home soft wood, it is not a success and is not worth the effort of carrying it. Always look for pieces that are mainly very hard. Small pieces of rotting wood can be removed but a piece that is mostly soft will probably continue to rot and is also difficult to clean.

PREPARATION OF THE DRIFTWOOD

There is very little wood that does not need some cleaning and polishing before it is used in a design.

Tools Required

A small, pointed knife, a wire brush and a scrubbing brush.

Cleaning

A good wash is needed before anything else. Scrub well with detergent and water, in a sink or a bath if the wood is large. Disinfectant may be necessary in some cases and an insecticide if there are insects and 'creepy-crawlies'.

Wash *grey wood* gently, without a scrubbing brush, as the greyness is only on the surface and will disappear with vigorous scrubbing.

Dry in the sunshine or any warm dry place.

Removal of Soft Wood

It is important to remove soft wood which rots and is dusty, and there will nearly always be small pockets of this in crevices. This job is easily done with the point of the knife. Bark may still cling to the wood and although this may be attractive if left on, it may also be removed with the knife. Stubborn bark may need soaking in water for a day before it can be removed. Broken twigs can be cut off with secateurs and larger branches with a saw. This part of the preparation is dirty and

Cleaning a piece of driftwood by brushing it with a strong wire brush

The wood is now ready for use. This piece makes a good container

should be done out of doors, in a workshop or on newspaper.

When the soft and broken wood has been removed, brush the piece all over with a strong wire brush bought at a hardware store or iron-mongers. This removes any soft wood on the surface and gives a good finish. Grey wood should not be brushed with anything except a very soft brush, otherwise the greyness will be lost.

Some people like a very smooth finish and this can be obtained with sandpaper; however, it can give a dull appearance and a lack of good textural quality. A sanding machine is even more drastic, producing a very smooth, if rather lifeless, appearance. Manzanita, which is usually grey and dark red in colouring, is cream underneath and is often sold like this after professional sanding.

After washing and brushing, or sanding, only the really hard wood should be left.

Altering the Shape

Removing wood. Branches, roots and stems can be pruned with secateurs. Crosscuts used for bases and flat pieces of wood can soon be shaped by a carpenter with a power saw. It is wise to take a paper pattern cut to the desired shape and temporarily pasted to the wood for the saw to follow, alternatively, a line may be pencilled on to the wood.

A scar is left whenever a saw is used on bigger chunks of wood and this should be disguised; it is not always easy as the inside of the wood is not the same colour as the outside. If possible use the wood as found, with only minor removals.

It is always wise to look at the wood for a few days, and at different angles, before a drastic re-shaping is undertaken. Often there is only a need for the addition of a small prop or leg, but at other times the shape is much improved, or the wood stands better, when part of it is removed. A sawing line can be made, to avoid errors, by lowering the wood into a bucket of water while holding it at the angle desired when finished. A tidemark should be left which the saw can follow or a chalk line may be drawn just above the water level.

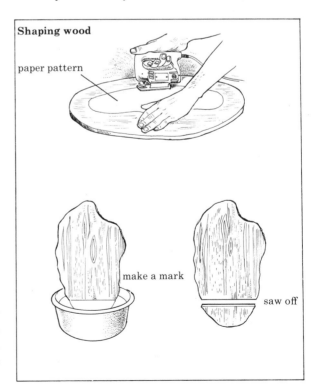

Shaping wood

paper pattern

make a mark

saw off

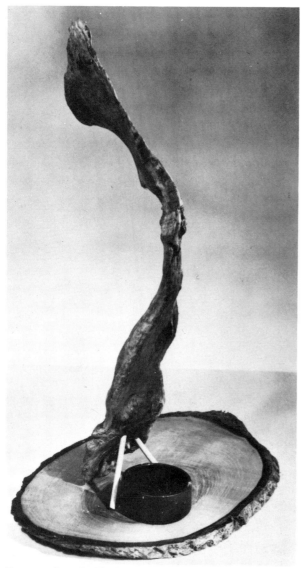

Two peg legs hold the wood upright. Flowers may be placed behind the wood in the well pinholder

Adding wood. It may be necessary to add a peg-leg or a small prop to hold larger chunks of wood in the correct position. A permanent prop is much more satisfactory than a temporary lump of Plasticine which may give way.

For a peg-leg, drill a hole in the wood to the same diameter as a piece of dowel from a 'Do-it-yourself' shop. Cut the dowel to the correct length *after* inserting it in the hole, to avoid mistakes. It is important that the angle of drilling is correct and the peg-leg points in the right direction. If it is loose in the hole a little glue may be necessary.

A screw can be used to fix a leg on to the main piece of wood but this is not normally as firm and the head of the screw needs disguising. Props may be added of small pieces of wood, preferably of the same type (perhaps from a part that has been removed), and either glued or screwed on.

Sometimes two or more smaller pieces of wood can be glued, or screwed, together to form one big, interesting piece.

Polishing

WAX. Wax is excellent, giving a gentle shine and protecting the surface. Furniture wax or shoe polish can be used. Brush the wax on liberally and then leave it for 24 hours for the wood to soak it up. Brush again for a shine, finishing with a soft cloth. If necessary repeat the process for a stronger shine.

VARNISH. Varnish provides complete protection from water but gives a harder appearance to the surface unless a matt varnish is used. Care should be taken over colour and the colourless varnishes are safer to use.

Grey wood should not be waxed or varnished as the greyness disappears.

Colouring

Often the colour of the wood, with soft mellow tones, is so beautiful in itself that no other treatment is necessary. However, sometimes the wood may be drab in colour or a special effect may be desired and there are several methods of changing the colour.

COLOURED SHOE POLISH. This may be used in place of colourless furniture wax or shoe polish. Try a small amount first, to be sure of the colour, on a hidden part of the wood.

STAIN. A wood stain may be used. This colours without giving a shine, but this can be added afterwards with colourless wax or polish.

PAINT. Matt paint can be applied with a brush. Black is effective but other colours can look lifeless. More interest can be given by wiping off some of the paint while it is still wet or by highlighting with a spray paint in another colour or with a metal finish. Alternatively, paint with three colours and then rub with steel wool to make them uneven.

Another method is to spray with an aerosol can of paint. This may be matt or shiny. Some of the wood can be left showing through. Alternatively, gold, silver or copper highlights can be added for interest.

LINSEED OIL. This darkens and preserves the wood but does not give a shine, which may be added afterwards with wax.

BLEACH. Bleach to a lighter colour by soaking the wood overnight in a bucket of water containing half a bottle of bleach. If the wood is too big for the bucket, place different sections in it and give each an overnight soak. Rinse when bleached and dry. This yellows the wood slightly. A solution of oxalic acid crystals (which are poisonous and must be kept out of the way of children), made by dissolving 1 tablespoonful in 1 quart of water, gives a pinker appearance. Soak the wood for about ten minutes and then rinse with hot water.

BLACKING. This can be effected with a blow-lamp or in a bonfire but the latter treatment may consume the wood completely unless care is taken! Wax may be applied afterwards and this 'settles the dust'. Black paint can also be used or black shoe polish.

SALT AND WATER. It will help to produce a grey effect if the wood is soaked in a bucket of water containing half a pound of salt. Dry in hot sunshine which assists bleaching considerably. This process may need to be repeated several times.

COLOURED CHALKS. These are good for touching up wood and concealing scars made by a saw. Rub the chalk well into the surface.

MECHANICS FOR DRIFTWOOD

When the wood is cleaned, altered, polished and perhaps coloured, it is ready for use in a design. It is essential that the wood is stable in an arrangement and as it is normally quite heavy care must be taken. The methods of supporting wood are not difficult and it is mainly a matter of choosing the best method for the kind of wood.

Branches, Stems and Roots

A pinholder. This will support lighter branches, roots and stems. It may be necessary to split the stem end with secateurs so that it goes easily on to the pins. Very light branches can be held in plastic foam.

A false leg. This makes a better support for branches with harder wood, heavy roots, heavy stems and pieces that need lengthening. It is attached by drilling a hole in the end of the piece of wood of the same diameter as a piece of dowel. Glue the dowel into the hole. Legs made from shorter lengths of dowel can then be placed on a pinholder (more than one leg may be necessary). If used in a tall container longer legs may be pushed into plastic foam, or sand, in the container. Heavy branches are not held securely in plastic foam without a false leg as the foam tears away and the wood falls out.

A clamp. One can be bought which holds quite heavy branches, stems and roots. The clamp, which screws tightly on to the wood, is built on to an 'upside-down' pinholder which fits firmly on to a normal pinholder. The clamp should be hidden with plant material but can be rather bulky to hide on occasions.

A screw. It is possible to buy a screw which is built into a heavy flat piece of lead. This will support medium weight branches, roots and stems on a base. The diameter of the stem end must be large enough to allow a hole of the same diameter

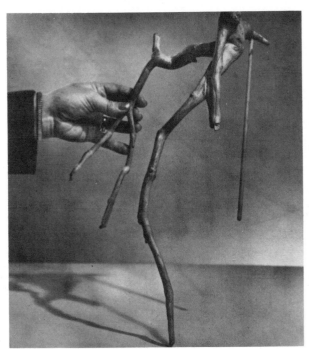

The stick on the right can be placed into a tall container to hold the wood in position

A clamp can be used to support heavy branches, stems and roots

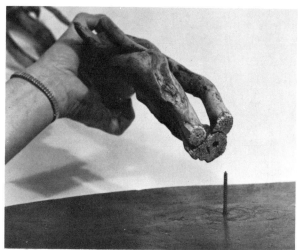

A large stem, such as ivy, can be held in place by means of a screw placed through a base

as the screw to be made in it. The hole can be made with a drill but take care to ensure that it is at the correct angle. The lead base may then be screwed on or off at will and the branch is held upright.

It is also possible to fix a screw pointing upwards through a flat wooden base. The screw should be countersunk so that furniture is not scratched and felt can be glued on to the bottom of the base for further protection. The driftwood should have a hole drilled in it of the same diameter as the screw. It can then be twisted on to the base at will. This is an excellent method as the base gives a firm support for the wood. A pinholder, in a tin, can then be placed near the wood for other plant material. Another advantage of this method is that the wood can be turned easily in any direction.

Plaster of Paris. This makes an excellent permanent support which is very stable. The only disadvantage can be in hiding it. It can be bought from a paint shop, chemist or drug store.

Put some of the powder in a bowl and then add water, stirring until the plaster starts to thicken. Very quickly push the lump of plaster on to a small sheet of polythene, mould it upwards and place in it the branch, stem or root. Hold it in position until the plaster sets, which only takes a few minutes, at the same time pushing the plaster upwards to support the wood. A hollow may be made in the plaster so that a well-type pinholder can be placed near to the wood for other plant material. When using the wood in an arrangement cover the plaster with moss or stones. It should be varnished to prevent water damage.

Plasticine. This is only suitable for very light branches and even these may fall out if the Plasticine gets warm.

Plaster of Paris makes a good permanent support for this large lichened branch

When used in an arrangement the plaster is hidden with moss and stones. Small iris give the impression of a pool

A twist of wood balances the exotic anthuriums and aspidistra leaves

These normally stand by themselves. If in need of propping up, a permanent leg or prop may be added, as described previously. A pinholder (upside down) or a heavy tin may be used as a temporary support.

Driftwood used for an elegant container on a Chinese base. It was polished with black shoe polish

Driftwood featured as sculpture. A piece of dowel was glued into both wood and plinth to hold it in place

Driftwood may be used successfully in many ways and with all types of plant material. There is, however, no point in using it and then hiding it behind other plant material. Restraint in adding flowers and leaves and plenty of space within the design are important qualities in any arrangement which uses driftwood.

For line. Branches, roots and woody stems are very useful plant material to use for a 'line' in an arrangement, especially in winter when other line plant material is in short supply. Combined with two or three flowers and a little foliage and using plenty of space in the design, driftwood provides an interesting and economical winter arrangement.

The plant material can be arranged in a well-type pinholder placed next to the wood and on a large base, possibly made from a crosscut of a tree trunk. Another piece of wood or a small amount of bark may be used to cover the pinholder.

As a container. Sometimes a large chunk of wood can be made into a container. The wood must be levelled so that it stands well, otherwise there will be water spillages, and then a hole can be made, or an existing hole enlarged, to hold a small tin for the water and mechanics. Occasionally a piece may be so elegant that it can be used on top of an antique stand or trivet. Other pieces may stand alone or on a wooden base and a tree stump is effective used as a container for a branch and flowers, especially with daffodils in the spring.

For bases. Crosscuts of wood make excellent bases and the bark may be left on if it is attractive. The wood should be well seasoned before it is placed in a warm room to avoid warping and a consequent lack of flatness. Crosscuts are especially suitable for use with other driftwood as there is a natural harmony between them.

As a cover-up. Small pieces of bark and driftwood are invaluable as they often fit well over the mechanics to hide them. This means that a design need not be cluttered at the base with lots of plant material used only for hiding the mechanics and not as part of the design. A much clearer, simpler effect is obtained in this way. It does not harm hard wood to place it in the container in water. The most useful small pieces of wood and bark are those which have a gentle curve to fit around the mechanics.

Featured as sculpture. A large piece of wood with a lovely shape and good colouring and texture can make a fascinating feature in a room, especially in a modern home. It can stand on furniture or in a niche, as a piece of 'sculpture' –

and is much less expensive. One never becomes tired of its ageless mellow quality. It may be mounted on its own small plinth in the same way as a sculpture.

For atmosphere. Wood is surprisingly interpretative, very quickly creating an atmosphere or setting the imagination working, so that one is transported to a bleak mountainside, a softer woodland or a windy March day by the shape and position of the wood. This makes it very useful for competitive flower arrangement shows in which one may be asked to give an interpretation or set an atmosphere, apart from also being of interest at home as a conversation piece.

Combining Wood with Plant Material

Fresh flowers and foliage. Almost all fresh plant material seems compatible with wood. Orchids are often used with it in America, roses in Britain, proteas in South Africa; the exotic anthuriums and strelitzia and, of course, more common flowers such as chrysanthemums, dahlias and so on, are all very easy to use with wood. Wild flowers seem especially suitable. The design itself should usually be restrained and rather natural in appearance to match the natural feeling of the wood, with the fresh plant material placed near the wood but not hiding it. Foliage can be used alone with wood, with great success.

Preserved plant material. Wood is plant material that has dried naturally and so it seems to have a natural harmony with dried and glycerined plant material. The bolder forms of preserved material are usually more successful than many fussy little ones because they should be in scale with the wood which is usually bold in shape. This is a most economical combination of materials for a winter arrangement as it is almost permanent. Alternatively, the wood can remain in place, with a simple change of other plant material for variety, and this makes a semi-permanent design.

Fruit. This blends well with wood as it seems to have the same sculptural qualities. It looks quite effective on a dining table if the wood is very clean and well polished. Varying colours, textures and shapes in the fruit give greater interest.

Plants. A grouping of plants in a container may have a piece of wood added. These again seem to have a natural affinity and the wood can provide needed height or a change of texture. It is also possible to put the roots of small plants in a polythene bag with compost and place them on a base with driftwood to hide the bags, but this is a less permanent way of combining wood and plants as the plants do not stay in good condition in a polythene bag.

Many happy hours may be spent looking for driftwood and then preparing it for use with other plant material or alone. Its versatility is quite amazing and it lasts for ever.

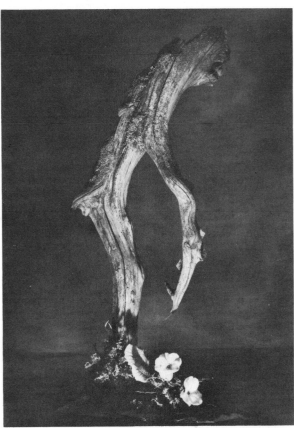

'Menace' – an arrangement of wood to evoke the atmosphere implied in the title

A design combining wood and fruit makes an appropriate centrepiece for the table

Above: The effect of a small area of brilliant colour with larger amounts of other colours. Gladioli, roses, carnations and tulips with alabaster grapes, driftwood and bleached and tinted aspidistra leaves in a Victorian plant pot

Opposite: A design in warm colours of roses, dahlias, hydrangeas and chrysanthemums. Such an arrangement is very effective in a sunless room or for providing a welcome on a cold day

Colour, Texture, Shape and Space

It is instinctive for us to like order in our environment – we tidy our homes and gardens and dislike our untidy cities. We also admire a sense of design in the objects about us and appreciate those that are well designed. It is quite natural then for us to prefer a flower arrangement that is satisfyingly ordered instead of a haphazard jumble of plant material.

Order takes many forms and this is the reason for the varying styles seen in flower arrangement, but whatever the style a good design has a sense of being thought about and pleasingly organised.

The art of organising or designing does not belong only to the arranging of flowers but is a foundation for all the visual arts. Basic design, once understood, can be applied to any medium that is used and this is why people who have had training in design in another field very quickly pick up the art of flower arrangement.

To learn about design we need to know about two things:

1. The qualities present in the medium in which we are working. In flower arrangement it is the unchanged, or little changed materials of nature, which can be assembled to give special effects.
2. The ways in which these qualities can be controlled and assembled together. These are called the design principles.

THE QUALITIES OF PLANT MATERIAL

A flower may be a good specimen of a camellia, of a specific variety, but in addition it has characteristics of interest to a designer – *colour, texture* and *shape*. All plant material, flowers, leaves, fruit, wood and so on, possesses these. Sometimes, as in the camellia, all three qualities are beautiful. At other times only one or two of these may be beautiful and the other nondescript, as in a piece of driftwood with exciting shape but ordinary texture and drab colour. Whether beautiful or not, these three qualities are present in all plant material and there is an infinite number of fascinating variations. The way these are combined together in a design is what flower arrangement is all about. For example, a flower arranger may pick a beautifully shaped branch which is placed in a container with a brilliant flower, to provide some colour, and two or three leaves for a contrast of texture. Each piece of plant material is thought about as it is placed in the container, with regard to its colour, texture and shape and its relationship with the other pieces of plant material as they are added. This knowledgeable selection and deliberate combination of various colours, textures and shapes makes harmonious and pleasing designs and 'lifts' flower arrangement from being merely a bunch of flowers in a vase.

All designers work with these particular qualities to a certain extent, but often more with one or two of them than with all three. The weaver is especially concerned with colour blending and with creating lovely textures with yarns, the sculptor with composing beautiful forms from marble, stone and metal and the painter with colour and shape. The flower arranger does not have as much power to change the 'raw' materials as the weaver, sculptor and painter and is concerned with the composing of materials ready to be immediately used, but it is still necessary to know something about colour, texture and shape to make a pleasing flower arrangement. This also helps when something distinctive noticed in the plant material is to be emphasised in order to bring it to the attention of others who look at the design.

The flower arranger is very dependent on the availability of plant material and cannot create a colour if it is not available, as a painter can with a few tubes of paint. However, the materials of flower arrangement are as endless as nature itself and with a variety of containers, bases and accessories there is also an endless variation of designs. In the summer there is almost too much choice and selection can be very difficult. The answer is to think about the design while picking (or buying) and to avoid haphazard cutting which can be wasteful. Think in terms of the arrangement and where it is to be placed in your home, the shapes that go well together, the colours to be blended and the textures to give interest. This makes choosing plant material very much easier, quicker and more economical. To be able to think 'arranging' when making a selection, it becomes necessary to know something of each of the three qualities, colour, texture and shape, and how to combine them so that they are pleasingly related.

COLOUR

The most powerful of the three qualities is colour. It can have great emotional effect and evokes considerable response in people. It has been loved in every civilisation: the Phoenician considered his purple dye to be priceless, the Chinese selected beautiful glazes for their fine porcelain, the Egyptians decorated their tombs with colour, many African nations love brilliant colours in their clothes and gypsies like it on their caravans. Paintings full of vibrant colour have existed since the earliest days and gardens have always been planted, and homes furnished, with colour as the main concern. It is probably true to say that the average homemaker's chief purpose in setting flowers in her house has been for the brilliance provided by their colour.

There are thousands of colours in the world – they can be rich, dull, brilliant, pale, subtle, weak, strong. The whole field of colour is very broad as so many people use it both for pleasure and because of the work they do. There are various theories about the use of colour and a lot of confusing terminology which sometimes makes a lovely subject tediously theoretical. As yet no universal basis for the use of colour has been agreed and those who regularly work with it have developed their own theory and terminology to suit their special needs. Flower arrangers also have special needs and interests, and it is wise to define these so that some limitation can be put on the broad field of colour. They are concerned with:
1. Combining existing colours (not mixing pigment) in plant material, containers, bases and accessories to give a pleasing effect.
2. Suiting the colours of the flower arrangement to the colours in the room so that the design and its setting are in harmony.
3. The way colours alter when placed in differing surroundings, when the lighting changes and when colours are used in varying amounts.
4. The use of colour to convey an atmosphere and appeal to the emotions and its strong powers of

A camellia has colour, texture and form

association, which are useful when entering interpretative classes at flower arrangement shows.

The interest of many flower arrangers in colour becomes highly developed through working with it in flower arrangement and it becomes a constantly exciting challenge. It always remains a very personal thing – people enjoy certain colours and combinations of colours more than others and there is nothing wrong in this as there are no rules for its use. There are, however, guide lines which have proved reliable. In order to understand these, some knowledge of existing colour terminology and one of the basic theories is useful but observation, practice and experiment are usually better teachers. Flower arrangers use a pigment theory as a basis.

Colour Description

Every colour can be identified by three qualities which are also called dimensions (or characteristics). They are a means of describing or measuring colours.

Hue. This quality refers to the type of colour and a name is given to distinguish it from other colours. Six are plainly evident – red, orange, yellow, green, blue, violet – although there are many in-betweens such as red-orange, orange-yellow and so on. When these colours are seen in

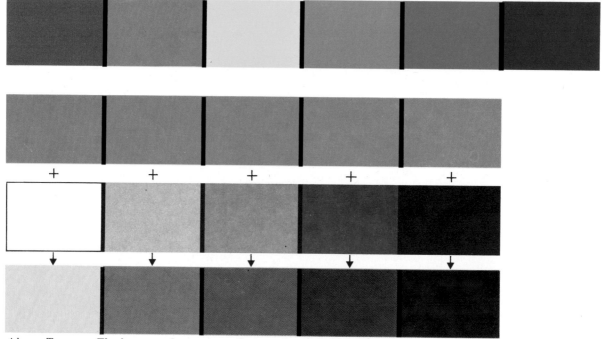

Above: Top row. The hues – red, orange, yellow, green, blue and violet. Three-row diagram. The addition of white, greys and black to the hue (orange) gives the tint, tones and shade shown in the bottom row

a rainbow they blend into each other in an un-broken line. For explanatory purposes it is simpler to separate the colours so that they can be named and distinguished.

The term hue refers to pure unmodified colours. They can be seen when light is refracted in the ·rainbow, a fountain, a dewdrop, a diamond or a chandelier. They can also be seen in many flowers such as an orange marigold, a red poppy, a yellow daffodil and in the feathers of some birds, wings of butterflies, stained glass windows and chemicals. Pure unmodified colours are rarer than other colours and this is probably a good thing as, though very beautiful, they can be tiring to the eye.

Value. This term, often referred to as tonal value, describes the second dimension or characteristic – that of lightness or darkness. Not all colours are pure hues and some are versions of a pure hue, and seem to contain black or white or to visually appear darker or lighter. A small experiment with a paint-box helps in understanding this. Mix two pools of pure red paint. To one add a little black paint – the result will be a darkened version of red (sometimes called maroon). To the other pool of red add a lot of white paint and the result will be a lightened version of red (pink).

The following terms are used:

SHADE. A hue with black added, or a darkened version of a hue.

TINT. A hue with white added, or a lightened version of a hue.

It is interesting to see in the diagram that brown is not a pure hue but a shade of orange,

apricot is a tint of orange and so on. Sometimes both black and white seem to be present in a colour with the hue having a greyed appearance. This may appear light or dark according to the amounts of white or black present. Try mixing another pool of red paint with both black and white which will give a greyed appearance. Add more white for a lighter greyed look and more black for a darker one.

TONE. A hue with black and white added or a greyed version of a hue. There are dark tones and light tones.

NEUTRALS. Black, white and grey are referred to as neutrals or achromatic colours. Chromatic colours are the hues. When achromatic and chromatic colours are mixed together in paint, the result is tonal values (or tints, tones and shades). There is no true black, white or grey in plant material. For example, most white flowers are a tint of another colour – a rose may be the palest pink, an arum is pale green, a chrysan-themum may be palest yellow. The black centres of tulips are usually blue-black or red-black.

Intensity. The third dimension or characteristic is one of saturation, in other words some colours seem to contain a lot of the hue and little or nothing of anything else. They are like a solution that has all the hue that is possible poured into it. They are said to be of high intensity. The pure hues seen in the rainbow or in a poppy are not modified in any way and are at maximum satura-tion. Other colours are of low intensity or satura-tion, for example, a piece of beige driftwood has almost no hue in it and is more saturated with

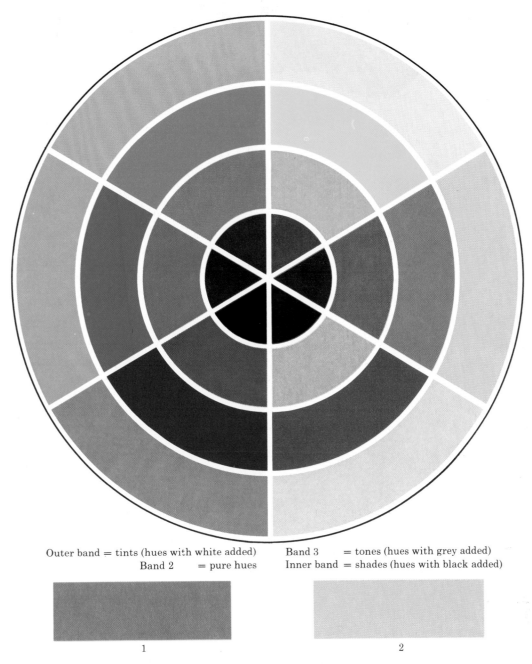

Outer band = tints (hues with white added) Band 3 = tones (hues with grey added)
Band 2 = pure hues Inner band = shades (hues with black added)

1

2

Top: A colour circle, only one tint, tone and shade of each hue is shown.
Bottom: Saturation 1. High intensity 2. Low intensity

greyness. It is *reduced* in intensity. Another term often used in place of intensity is chroma. Colours of low intensity are often very beautiful and we are very aware of them in the British Isles where there are many. They include all the smokey, soft and pearly colours such as those seen on a misty autumn morning, during twilight or dawn, in weathered stone and doves' feathers.

'Than these November skies is no sky lovelier
The clouds are deep;
Into their grey the subtle spies of colour creep.'
John Freeman

Neutralised colours. Colours of low intensity

are often named in this way because there is only a tinge of hue present which is scarcely definable. These colours are easy to blend with others because their 'personality' is not strong and they offer no great competition. They are excellent colours for backgrounds, bases, and containers for this reason, and they do not vie with the flowers.

A colour, then, is measured or described by three terms which relate to the hue, the tonal value, and the intensity. There is an infinite number of each, and of their combinations, in the world, which is often the reason for colour selection being a difficult matter.

Colour Names

Various ways of naming colours have been evolved, based on these three dimensions, but it is easier for most people to use names which have been given because of association – such as sky blue, pillar-box red, raspberry pink, forest green, golden yellow. It is a little more accurate to call mushroom pink a tint of red with low intensity, but it is doubtful if there will ever be universal acceptance of such terms, especially when the associative names are so expressive.

Colour Relationship

Any help in selecting and combining colours is useful for flower arrangement and it is possible to trace relationships between colours if the hues are placed in a circle with one tint, one shade and one tone of each. Although only one of each is used for practical reasons there are, in reality, an infinite number.

The colours should be placed logically in sequence as shown. Yellow and red make orange when mixed in paints, and orange should be placed between them. Similarly, violet which is mixed from red and blue, and green which is mixed from blue and yellow.

Any colours may be combined which a designer enjoys and there are *no rules* but there are certain colour combinations which are pleasing to many people as the colours seem to be related. These are called *basic colour schemes* and they can be understood by looking at the colour circle.

Monochromatic. This refers to tints, tones and shades of one colour such as those shown in the orange segment. When colours from the adjacent yellow or red segments are used, the colour scheme is no longer monochromatic. This combination of colours can be very restful and is a useful one for a flower arranger to use against a highly patterned wallpaper. It can also be uninteresting, unless extremes are used in value, such as apricot and dark brown instead of two closely related oranges. Contrasts in the texture and form of the plant material also add more interest. Flowers and leaves are rarely one colour – flowers may have yellow centres, green stems and leaves or be of many colours, as some hydrangeas. Leaves may show a streak of yellow or red. It is, therefore, sensible to aim for a general impression or *predominance* of one colour rather than to try to adhere exactly to a monochromatic scheme in flower arrangement. Otherwise it is not a realistic scheme to use. In fabrics and furnishings it is very much easier.

Adjacent. This is a popular combination of colours for flower arrangement because it is easy. It uses colours which are adjacent to each other on the colour circle – yellow and orange, orange and red, red and violet, violet and blue, blue and green, green and yellow, together with all the tints, tones and shades of each that are desired. The colours seem related because, in each pair, one of the colours contains a lot of the other colour. This can also be seen more easily when paints are mixed together. Mix yellow and red paint together. This will give orange which is closely related to both yellow and to red. There is no need to keep to only two colours in an adjacent colour scheme, yellow, orange and red may be used, for example, but these seem more related if the red is an orange-red or the yellow an orange-yellow, and not leaning towards a blue-red or a green-yellow.

Complementary. Colours which lie opposite to each other on the colour circle also have a relationship – that is red and green, yellow and violet, blue and orange. This can be seen if you look at a red circle for a long time and then close your eyes, when a green circle will be seen. (The same thing happens with the other opposite colours to a lesser extent.) The eye, tiring of red, sees green as a relief. It follows that if red and green are seen together the combination is satisfying. Opposite colours have the power to intensify each other when used together. So much so that a green and a red of equal strength will be too much for the eyes and it is better to use a dark green with a light red.

Triadic. This refers to the use of three colours equidistant apart on the colour circle. For example, yellow, blue and red. Again it is more attractive to use these in unequal strength with, perhaps, a medium amount of a dark tone of red with a lot of blue tint and an accent of golden yellow. This combination of colours – yellow, red and blue – has often been used by great painters.

Polychromatic. In flower arrangement this term refers to the use of many colours together, as is seen in a bouquet of garden flowers. This can be more tiring on the eye than other colour combinations and so it is often better to use colours with less intensity. The Flemish and Dutch flower paintings are good examples.

These basic colour combinations, or schemes, are useful knowledge but often it is the choice of the modified colour which is of greater importance than the hue chosen – meaning the tint, shade or tone, rather than the type of colour. It is true also that lighting, surroundings and the amount of each colour often have greater significance.

Inspiration

The colour circle is useful for explanations but is not in itself very inspiring and there are many other things in the world around us which give ideas for colour schemes.

Nature. Beautiful combinations of colours may be seen in flowers, leaves, birds, animals, shells, precious stones, rocks, skies, weather, mountains, moorlands and seashore. It is worth taking time to really look at the feathers of a chaffinch, the pearly colours in a shell, the rich hues of a pansy, a brilliant sunset, a misty morning, a rocky pool. These colours can be stored in your mind, or roughly recorded with paint in a notebook, to provide endless inspiration for colour combinations in flower arrangement.

Paintings. The artist is usually a brilliant colourist because the primary concern is with colour. It is helpful to study the amount of each colour used, the tonal values, the many variations of one colour, the combination of warm and cool colours, the atmosphere that can be created through colour.

Designers. Stage and television settings and costumes, tapestries, shop windows, advertisements, clothes, fabrics, pottery, china, and furnishings can all give ideas and inspiration.

Colour Variation

There are many different colours in plant material and, unless a quiet colour scheme is needed, it is a pity not to include the lovely variations which exist. Pick a bunch of leaves and notice how many greens there are – blue and yellow greens, soft and hard greens, dark and light greens, greyed greens, brilliant and dull greens. An arrangement which contains several of these usually has much more vitality and interest than a design with only one, as, for example, plain green hosta leaves with bright pink roses. The addition of a variegated hosta leaf showing more than one green will usually give life to the arrangement.

Flowers often change colour with age – some red roses can become very blue as they get older – and leaves can develop streaks of red, yellow and brown, especially in autumn. These variations give a vibrant and moving quality to a design.

Colour Repetition

Unexpected colours can be combined if each colour is repeated somewhere else in the design. Here again the Flemish and Dutch flower paintings are worthwhile studying. Some plant material is excellent for linking together two seemingly unlike colours – for example, red and blue seem to have little relationship, but can be combined if hydrangea flowers containing both colours (and perhaps violet) are added to the design.

Colour Temperature

Colours can appear warm or cool and this is usually a matter of association. Red and orange seem to be warm, reminding us of a fire, and blue and green, the colours of water and sky, seem cooler. Violet and yellow are colours which can look either warm or cool depending on their surroundings. Yellow, for example, will look warm with red and orange but cool when with blue and green. Many painters like a combination of warm and cool colours as each enhances the other.

Knowledge of colour temperature is useful for flower arrangement when considering surroundings. A room with little sunshine may need a warm-coloured flower arrangement and an all-green room may look wonderful with a red accent of flowers. On a cold day a warm red-orange arrangement will provide a better welcome than a cool blue and green one, which is more appropriate for hot weather.

Luminosity

Some colours are more visible than others in poor light. White and tints (that is hues mixed with white), yellow, yellow-green and orange have higher luminosity than other colours. Black and violet are the least luminous and in poor lighting may disappear completely. The luminosity of white can be so strong that it can disturb a design – a white flower, amongst flowers of other colours, can appear far too dominant, as can a white container. In this case it is helpful to use some white flowers as a link with the container.

In dark corners of a room or when dining by candlelight, which is very weak, the most luminous colours should be used if there is to be any impact at all from the flowers.

Lighting

Lighting alters colours considerably, and it is seldom consistent. It changes with the time of the day, the season, the amount of sunshine, in the presence of various types of artificial lighting. Within just one room, lighting varies and you

Above: Inspiration for the colour of this arrangement comes from the pattern on the curtains
Opposite: An unusual colour scheme of pink Queen Anne's Lace, *Paeonia delavayi*, and maple

have only to look at the walls of a room to see this – the colour may appear quite different on each wall although the same can of paint was used on all four walls.

White fluorescent lighting makes reds appear brown and dull. Warm white fluorescent lighting helps to make reds more normal. Strong daylight enhances blues, and tungsten (electric lighting but not fluorescent) enhances reds, yellows and oranges. Any colours chosen for the home should be considered at all times of day and in all forms of lighting. The light in churches is normally rather dim and so it follows that colours with high luminosity will show up better than other colours.

Colour Movement

Some colours give the impression of being closer to the viewer than others. Orange, red and yellow seem to advance while blue and violet tend to recede and green is neutral in movement. This is only a generalisation as it is dependent also on the value and intensity of the colour concerned and the texture. A shiny orange poppy will seem closer to the viewer than a shaggy orange chrysanthemum.

This is useful knowledge when decorating a large room or hall which will need advancing colours if the flowers are to show up well. Small rooms may often be more pleasing when receding colours are used in the flowers.

Weight Quality

Colours can appear 'light' or 'heavy' according to their tonal value. For example, tints such as apricot seem light in weight whereas maroon looks heavy. All tints have less weight than shades because of the white content. Normally two colours of equal weight do not enhance each other, for example, when a dark bronze chrysanthemum is combined with dark green foliage. A more pleasing design results from using the dark green foliage with lighter orange flowers.

Colour Areas

Most people find that smaller areas of pure colour are more acceptable and less tiring to the eyes than larger amounts. In the British Isles most people are happier living with colours of less intensity as the brilliant ones can appear harsh in surroundings misted by humidity and the lack of clear skies. In hotter, drier countries larger areas of pure colour may be more acceptable. Landscapes give examples of small areas of brilliant colour with larger areas of duller colour – poppies in a cornfield; a few bright flowers in a garden of green foliage, grass and brown earth; heather on a mountainside.

A general guide, although much depends on the lighting and surroundings, is to use least of the most brilliant colours in a group and more of the paler and duller colours. Sometimes one colour in a design may stand out too much amongst the others, in which case it should be removed for a better overall effect.

Colour Surroundings

Colour cannot be isolated from surrounding colours, which can change the effect. For example, a grey leaf looks grey against green wallpaper but when placed in front of grey wallpaper it can look green. Lighting also alters colours and the result of these outside influences is an ever-changing, moving, kaleidoscopic quality. This 'vibration' can be both exciting and frustrating. An arrangement done at home in clear daylight may look quite different when placed in a tent with duller lighting, or in a room with fluorescent lighting. There are a few guide lines which are helpful:
1. Colour seen against mid-grey probably appears at its truest.
2. Warm colours look warmer when placed against cool colours and the same is true of cool colours in front of a warm background – they will look cooler.
3. Light colours appear lighter against a dark background and vice versa. Flowers with strong contrasts in tonal value also give a greater sense of space between them.
4. Colours appear more brilliant against their complement, for example, red against green.
5. A colour can look duller or more brilliant according to its background. For example, red may seem really bright in front of beige but quite dull against a brilliant orange.

It is useful to make an arrangement and then try it against various coloured papers or fabrics to see the effect. Studying the background colours of photographs is also helpful.

The Personality of Colour

Colour has tremendous expressiveness, which is quite its most fascinating quality for most people. It can establish an atmosphere of richness, poverty, activity, tranquillity, gaiety, sadness, drama, daintiness, fantasy and so on. Study the work of great colourists such as Turner, Gauguin,

Constable, Rembrandt, to see how they have used colour to create an atmosphere and convey an effect.

Very often association on the part of the viewer plays an important part, such as blue and green which may give an air of tranquillity through association with sky and sea. Yellow may be associated with sunshine, youth, happiness. Most colours have both good and bad associations such as red, which can look warm and cheerful but can also be a danger signal.

When interpreting an idea or a subject in a class at a flower arrangement show, colour can be a great help for conveying an atmosphere and giving 'the message' to the judge, who probably has similar associations in mind. The title 'Youth' could be interpreted with yellow-green as this is associated by everyone with the first growth of plants in the spring.

Practical Arrangements

Practise the use of colour by creating the following arrangements:

(A) An arrangement to harmonise with a piece of fabric or some wallpaper or curtains in your home.

(B) Analyse the colours in a painting and reproduce them in a flower arrangement.

(C) A design which mixes warm and cool colours.

(D) A design to give an atmosphere of any one of the following – richness, subtlety, anger, drama, gaiety, tranquillity.

(E) A design inspired by the colours in any of the following – a shell, a piece of china, a flower, a sunset, dawn, moorland, the seashore.

(F) An arrangement for candlelight or a dark corner.

TEXTURE

Texture is a very sensuous quality and is closely connected with the feel of things. A child touches everything to find out how it feels through his fingers, but as he grows older his eyes will tell him the feel without actually touching. By looking he will know that fur is soft, velvet is downy, stone is hard and so on. Many textures are so lovely that even when we know how they will feel, they are still inviting to touch – smooth wood and bronze, lovely silks and tweeds.

Flower arrangements are not made to be touched and it may seem surprising that flower arrangers are concerned with texture, but objects can have textural quality and an appearance of roughness or smoothness, without being touched.

Rough textured proteas in a rough pottery container with a smooth inside

This textural quality may be pleasing or not and most people like to rub their hands over smooth driftwood but not over a prickly thistle!

The way textures are combined can also be pleasing or of little interest. In recent years the use of interesting textures has become more important in many fields of design. A room with a rough carpet, silk curtains, velvet chairs and satin cushions is far more fascinating than one where all textural surfaces are similar. And so it is with flower arrangement – when textures are carefully selected as well as colours, and put together in certain ways, the result is far more attractive than when textures are combined haphazardly without thought.

Objects have a textural feel and a textural look and usually these are the same. Sometimes they can be quite different – for example, a marigold feels silky but visually appears rough. The way the surface of the object is formed gives the visual texture.

Varieties of Texture

Flower arrangers, then, are mainly concerned with the textural appearance of plant material (visual texture) and there are many lovely examples. Think of the following:

downy peaches
satiny poppies
pansies like velvet
grapes with a bloom
leathery rhododendron leaves
sticky horse chestnut buds
prickly teasels
thorny rose stems
crinkly rhubarb leaves
glossy magnolia leaves
cauliflowers
fluffy dandelion seed heads

Texture is a lovely quality to study for flower arrangement because of the many differences in plant material.

Combining Textures

Texture is not such a dominant quality as colour and, although it should be considered just as much, there is a difference between the way textures and colours are combined. Colours are selected for their *relationship* and because they suit each other – but textures are selected for their *differences*. Contrasts in texture are more effective than likenesses. These contrasts seem to enhance each other and emphasise the particular quality, for example, a shiny apple looks more effective with a dull leaf than with a shiny one, but a downy peach is enhanced by a shiny leaf. Nature shows many of these delightful contrasts – the magnolia tree has leaves with a felty underneath and a shiny top; pussy willow has smooth stems and fluffy catkins.

There are also examples of contrasting textures when tiny delicate flowers grow in the crevices of rocks; with ferns near a still pool; rough cliffs with a smooth sea and in a rose with its thorny stem.

A few distinct and contrasting textures used together are more effective than many closely related ones, which seem monotonous. The two main groups of texture are rough and smooth. A combination of these in a design is always stimulating, such as a little rough sedum mixed with roses or a smooth beech leaf with a rough seed head.

Combining textures in a flower arrangement means combining not only the textures of the plant material but also of the container, base and perhaps the accessory. All belong to the total effect and the plant material cannot be isolated. For this reason a shiny copper container can enhance rough textured dried plant material such as achillea or pine cones.

The greatest contrasts in texture are needed in:
(A) Dried plant material arrangements which tend to be monotonous with many similar textures.
(B) Monochromatic (one-colour) designs where there can be little variety in colouring.
(C) Modern designs which use little plant material and in which strong contrasts give a more dramatic effect.
(D) Arrangements of fruit and vegetables which may have a repetition of similar forms. This can be dull without strong textural contrasts. For example, an orange probably looks better with a shiny apple than with a grapefruit of similar texture. There are so many lovely textures in fruit that good contrasts are easy to obtain – a gaze in the greengrocer's window is very rewarding.

Textural Effects

Although texture is a less dominant quality than colour or shape it can alter the effect of a design surprisingly. For example, a coloured glass container attracts the eye immediately because it reflects light so strongly. Flowers placed in such a container may hardly be noticeable unless they are bold and brilliant in colour to offset the attraction of the glass.

In the same way a shiny camellia leaf is more eye-catching than a dull green beech leaf. All shiny textures attract the eye more quickly and should be used carefully.

Texture also has an influence on colour and the two cannot be disassociated. For example, a flower such as a yellow dahlia with many petals will seem to have many more tonal values than a buttercup with a few smooth petals. Although the two flowers may be the same shade of yellow the rough texture of the dahlia will give the illusion of a darker yellow flower.

When objects are grouped together there is a different textural effect than when one of the objects is seen alone, for example, a flower seed may appear smooth and shiny but when many of the seeds are grouped together – perhaps in a seed collage – then the effect is of a rough textured area.

Association and Texture

People associate certain textures with ideas or other subjects – for example, roughness is often

'Sea Fantasy' is the title of this arrangement which illustrates the use of contrasts in textures

Narcissus are not easy to arrange as they are strong points. Turning the flowers helps

associated with masculinity, informality, frugality and smoothness with femininity, elegance, richness. A shiny surface can convey gaiety, a dull one sadness, and so on. These associations, in the same way as colour associations, are useful for interpretative classes at flower arrangement shows and help to convey an atmosphere to the judge and other viewers. In other words both colour and texture can be symbolic.

Practical Arrangements

Practise the use of texture with the following:
(A) A design featuring fruit and using varying textures.
(B) A foliage arrangement using shiny, dull and rough textured leaves.
(C) An arrangement in a glass container.
(D) An arrangement of dried material in a shiny metal container.

(E) A design which includes shiny shells and rough coral.
(F) A design interpreting cruelty or gaiety or contrasts.

SHAPE

The word shape refers to the outline of an object. It may also be called form. There are many lovely shapes in plant material – think of a lily and a rose, pine cones and gourds, the stems of ivy and the tendrils of sweet peas, the leaves of *Begonia rex* and aspidistra, the seed heads of poppies and lotus. Plant material has an infinite number of beautiful shapes which may be rounded as an apple, long and graceful as a reed, oval as many leaves. They may be solid as an orange, or contain space as an arum lily; they may be regular or irregular, geometrically shaped or free of a geometric form. Most shapes in plant material are three dimensional having depth as well as breadth and height, although some plants do have very flat, almost two-dimensional foliage. In flower arrangement these three-dimensional shapes are composed into a three-dimensional design. Usually the only two-dimensional type of flower arrangement is a pressed flower picture.

Basic Shapes

With so many variations of shape in plant material it can be difficult to select the ones that go well together in a design and for this reason a very general classification is helpful. This can make the choice in a flower shop or garden a little easier. There are three groups into which most plant material can be placed – rounded plant material, long or linear plant material and in-between, near-oval shapes. They are shown on page 31 but need more explanation.
Point. In designers' terminology a rounded or nearly rounded shape is referred to as a 'point'. It is the most compelling shape – think of the sun, a full moon, stars, traffic lights, people's eyes. All these compel your attention. This is why this shape is often used in advertisements to attract your eye and put over the most important message. In the same way, open rounded flowers also attract the attention more strongly than other shapes and they are often brilliant in colour, which is an added attraction. For these reasons they become the star performers in a flower arrangement – attracting more notice than anything else – and this is right and proper because they are usually very beautiful. Fruits such as

oranges and apples are also points but there are not many examples in foliage although echeveria and houseleeks, which grow in a rosette shape, can be classed as points. It is possible to make a point in plant material by twisting cane and reeds into a circle and fixing them so that they enclose space. This can still be termed a point although it is not solid in the centre.

Because points are so dominant and attract the eyes before any other shapes, they need to be used with restraint and care. A design which uses all points – that is flowers all facing full on – can be monotonous and lacking in rhythm or movement. When nothing but points in plant material is available, which can often happen, it is more attractive to turn some of the flowers so that they do not appear as a point. It is also helpful to use different sizes of point to give variety.

Regular spaces between points can be monotonous and there is more interest when the spaces are varied with some flowers closer to each other and others further apart. The balance of the design is better in many arrangements when the flowers in the centre are closer together than those on the outside.

When points touch each other, or are crowded together, the result is a massed effect which emphasises colour and texture but not individual shapes. These can only be seen when there is space around each one or when there is a different coloured background, when a light flower is placed against a darker one. If points are placed regularly in a row they tend to move the eye along instead of holding it in one place, for example, a row of carnations placed in an arrangement.

Points are very useful in a design as they are stabilisers or anchors – they hold the eye whereas other shapes move them along. Too much movement can make a restless design and most people are happier to have a place to which their eyes can return and rest from their wanderings around the remainder of the arrangement. Points provide this emphasis. More traditional flower arrangements use points, that is larger rounded flowers, in the centre of the design and they do provide a very good 'pivot point'. Smaller flowers or turned points are used at the extremities. Modern designers use points anywhere in the design to give good balance. This may be at the top of the arrangement or anywhere else the designer chooses, and where something dominant and emphatic is wanted.

The positions where points are used in a design, as resting places for the eyes or for emphasis, may be called focal points, centres of interest, emphasis points or areas of dominance.

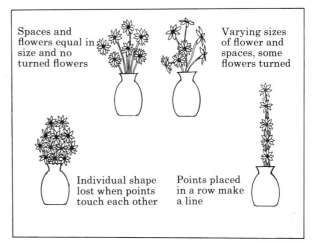

Points used to achieve various effects

Lines are very expressive and can be of many varieties each giving a different effect

Line. This is also a variety of shape, although it is so important in a design that some experts consider it under a separate heading. The term line refers to shapes which move the eyes along and do not hold them in one place, as points. Lines are used in a design to give movement and rhythm. There are many varieties – thick and thin, straight and curved, complicated and simple, delicate and bold. Their common characteristic is their ability to move the eyes, whether this is slowly or quickly. Sometimes lines are continuous and direct, such as a branch of a tree, but they can also be formed by placing other shapes in a row so that the eyes are moved along.

Lines have more power of expression than points and for this reason can create an atmosphere or give a feeling. They can give the impression of speed or of slowness, they can be active or passive, lazy and wandering, or vigorous. A flash of lightning is a very active line, a stream wandering through a meadow is a very lazy one. A straight upright line gives a sense of rigidity or dignity, as a soldier standing at attention. A straight horizontal line is peaceful and quiet, as a man lying asleep. Diagonal straight lines have speed like a man leaning forward as he runs. Curved lines can give a feeling of grace and playfulness. The expressive quality of lines can be used to make designs which interpret a subject, for example, twisting curved branches can be arranged to look like a March day when a strong wind is blowing.

In-between shapes. Many shapes can be classified as point or line but there are some which do not fit either classification as they neither hold the eyes as a point nor move them as a line. No good name has yet been found for these shapes but they are very useful. They are the peacemakers, the transitionals or stepping stones, which lessen the great contrast between the other two shapes. Often they can be called oval and the garden has many examples – laurel leaves, rose foliage, flower buds. Some designs, such as the more modern ones, use only points and lines, giving a sharper, more dramatic design, whereas traditional arrangements tend to use more points and transitional shapes and few lines and this gives a softer style of design.

Combining Shapes

The way these three shapes are combined gives different styles of flower arrangement. All three may be used alone, with one other shape, or with the two other shapes, depending on the material available and the effect desired.

An arrangement of all points is more static than one using all lines, which can appear very active. The amount of space used with the shapes also changes the style of design. The more space used within the design, the more individual shapes can be seen and enjoyed separately. The opposite of this style is a closely packed cone where the individual shapes are hardly seen but the outline of the cone is strong and more important than the parts which make it up. In between these two extremes is a style where both the outline and individual shapes are clear. This style uses a little space around each flower or a different colour behind each one to show the shape, for example, a bright flower can be placed in front of a dull green leaf and it will still show up clearly.

Arrangements for use in a church need a strong contour in order to show up well from a distance and in dimmer lighting. Individual flower and leaf shapes are less important and the effect needed is one of colour and bold outline. At other times arrangements may be made to be seen more closely, in a room at home, and then individual shapes within the design should be seen easily and will provide great interest.

Practical Arrangements

Practise the use of the three basic shapes:
(A) A design using all points, such as open dahlias. Turn some flowers away from the centre.
(B) A design which uses enclosed spaces as points, such as cane wired in loops.
(C) An arrangement of all line plant material.
(D) A cone-shaped design. This can be made from a triangle of $\frac{1}{2}$-in. mesh wire netting bent over with the sides wired together and stuffed with plastic foam or wet moss. Plastic foam for use with dried plant materials can be bought in a cone shape.
(E) A traditional triangular design using the largest, rounded flowers in the centre and smaller ones on the outside.
(F) An arrangement with a strong outline, for a church.
(G) A modern design with a large flower at the top which uses a lot of space within the design.

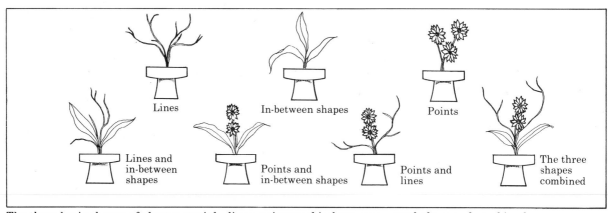

The three basic shapes of plant material – lines, points and in-betweens – used alone and combined

84

(H) Interpretative arrangements of lightning, a windy day, a dance, a piece of music, which use line plant material to express the subject.

SPACE

Space cannot be touched in the same way as colour, texture, and shape and it is not a quality which is present in plant material unless you count the space inside flowers. However, space is a 'material' or quality that designers must consider. Without space, shapes cannot be seen clearly. Objects pushed together on a rubbish heap have no clear individual forms but all contribute to one large untidy form with an irregular outline. A piece of sculpture shows up well against an open sky, a painting is more easily seen, well lit, on a bare wall, the branches of a tree are more visible when it grows alone in an open field than when grouped with other trees in a forest. Space and shape are necessary to each other, as we can only know one because of the other.

Until recently the Western world has not been as conscious of the value of space in design as the Eastern world, where all art, including that of flower arrangement, has always used a lot of space as part of any design. Massed flower arrangements are traditional in Europe, but in recent years greater restraint in the use of plant material, and far more space within the design itself, has become a popular trend.

Working with Space

This may sound odd, but a flower arranger should be as conscious of the spaces created when solid flowers are placed in a container as of the flowers themselves! Space helps to create the pattern of the design. It is also important to think of the space in which the flower arrangement will

An uncluttered design shows the plant material to its best advantage

be placed in a room and design it accordingly. **The space of the setting.** Most flower arrangements are made to be put in certain places in a room – perhaps on a mantelpiece, side table, windowsill, chest of drawers. The boundaries of the space available for the flower arrangement are made by the furniture and furnishings. A chest of drawers may have a picture over it and a lamp standing on it and neither should be hidden by the flowers which should fit into the remaining space. A mantelpiece may need a long, low central arrangement because of a painting over it and perhaps ornaments at each end. The 'block' of

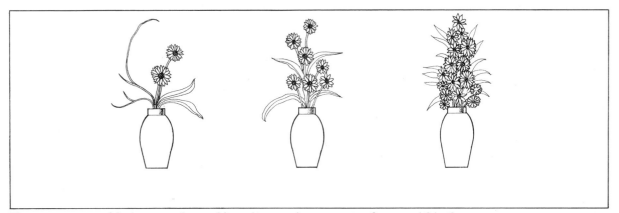

The appearances of designs are changed by using varying amounts of space within them

The stems are kept close together in a column to achieve a fan-like effect at the top of the design

clearly seen. When a flower is placed in front of a branch of driftwood then the wood cannot be seen so it is better to place the remaining plant material in any of the spaces left. Some modern designs deliberately use space in a pattern by enclosing it with plant material.

Space below the plant material. Arrangements need not sit directly on the table with the plant material touching the top of the table, but can be lifted up by means of a stemmed or footed container, pedestal or stand. Those that bring the plant material very close to the table top, for example in a well-type container on a base, tend to look heavier than those which are raised. When the plant material is lifted, the lower placements can be seen more clearly and graceful curves can be used at the lower sides of the design.

Another lovely way of using space, below the most important pieces of plant material, is to keep the stems very close together in a column arising from the container so that the flowers or leaves fan out towards the top of the design. This is a technique often seen in both classical and modern Japanese flower arrangements and it gives an especially light and active effect.

space which remains will suggest the shape and the size of the design. A tall narrow space needs a tall narrow arrangement. A wider, but still tall, space needs a wider, flowing design and a coffee table may need a low, horizontal arrangement.

Space within the design. The various styles of flower arrangement use differing amounts of space within the design. Mass arrangements use little and line arrangements use a lot. When making a mass design the arranger leaves a little space around each flower – there is a charming Japanese saying 'Leave room for the butterflies to fly through'.

In a line arrangement the space needs more consideration and all the plant material needs a lot of space around it so that each shape can be

Practical Arrangements

Practise the use of space:
(A) A design in a pedestal container.
(B) An arrangement for a chosen position in your home. Draw a rough plan of the available space before starting.
(C) A massed arrangement using a little space around each flower.
(D) A line arrangement using a branch or a piece of driftwood with the flowers placed away from the wood so that it is not hidden.
(E) A design which frames one flower by enclosing it in a framework of branches, driftwood or foliage.
(F) A line design – then turn it into a mass design by adding more plant material.

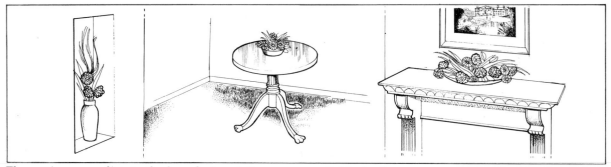

The settings may dictate the boundaries of the spaces available for the arrangements and affect their shapes and sizes

Design for Flower Arrangers

Grouping lovely colours, textures and shapes with care, and considering the spaces between the flowers, are not quite all that a flower arranger needs to know in order to create good designs. There are other considerations, which in designers' terms are called *the design principles*. These are abstract and not tangible as are colour, texture and shape, but they are not hard to understand and soon become part of the flower arranger's sub-conscious mind. You may hardly be aware of them and yet the guidance is there.

These design principles are basic to all the arts and a foundation on which to base new styles, they are the 'rocks' under the changing fashions and are universal and timeless. They are based on nature and have been formalised into words by experts in aesthetics who, in studying objects that have been considered beautiful through the centuries such as Michelangelo's David, Botticelli's Birth of Venus, Chinese porcelain, Persian rugs, have determined certain qualities common to them all. It has been generally agreed that pleasing scale and proportions, good balance, a sense of rhythm, areas that are emphasised in the design and some degree of contrast are present in all man-made things that have beauty. There are small rules that are sometimes used in teaching flower arrangement which may give 'instant' flower arrangement for a few set styles, but which give no real understanding of what makes good design and are no substitute for knowledge of the design principles.

Studying the design principles, for the purpose of creating good flower arrangements, also has another advantage: it leads to greater understanding, and therefore pleasure, of all design – paintings, sculpture, furniture, household articles – because the design principles are common to all good design in any field.

SCALE

Scale is easy to understand as we are all quick to recognise when a table is too big for a room, a hat too small for a large woman, a tree too big for a small garden. In the same way small flowers look wrong in a big container and large ones in a small container. However, size is relative – an object seen by itself is not big or small until it is seen next to another object for comparison. If there is a great difference between them the objects do not sit happily together. In flower arrangement there are many separate objects – flowers, leaves, container, base, accessory – and these all need to be related in size without a strong contrast.

1. Each piece of plant material should be related in size to the others, for example, a hydrangea and a violet are unhappy partners.
2. The plant material should be related in size to the container – a large peony would look wrong in a wine glass.
3. The base should not be either too big or too small for the rest of the design. A common fault is to use one that is too large.
4. The accessory, if used, should be in scale with the remainder of the design and not seem huge or dwarfed.
5. The whole design should be in scale with its setting. For example, a church needs big arrangements and a cathedral needs ones almost too big to create. A hospital locker needs small designs and a dining-room table needs a flower arrangement which also leaves room for food and china and does not inhibit conversation.

There are certain styles of flower arrangement which need more attention to scale. These are described on page 88.

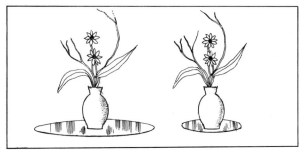

Left: Base out of scale with the arrangement. *Right:* Base of a better size

The Chinese figurine, twig and flowers are carefully scaled to give a life-size appearance

Landscape Designs

This is the name given to a group of designs which are copies of natural scenes such as a corner of a woodland, lakeside or mountain – a moment from nature. They are realistic natural scenes and for this reason should be scaled in the natural scale of life. For example, a figurine of a man standing next to a twig (representing a tree) should be related in size as a real tree is to a real man.

Practical Arrangements

To increase awareness of good scale practise:
(A) A landscape design which scales everything as the natural scale.
(B) A 'water' arrangement in which plant material which grows in water is arranged in a low bowl.
(C) A pedestal arrangement using large plant material.
(D) A miniature arrangement in a tiny container.
(E) A large arrangement to be seen from a distance in a church.
(F) A design for a dinner table.

PROPORTION

Although each flower and leaf may be in scale with the container and also well related to each other, too many flowers and leaves may be used so that the container is overwhelmed with plant material. This is not a matter of 'too small' or 'too large' but of 'too much'. Good proportion refers to pleasing amounts of things and again it is a matter of relationship. The same amount of plant material which appears too much for one container may seem quite correct for another one. Scale concerns *relative sizes* and proportion concerns *relative amounts*. A number of arrangements can be made in a room and all may be in scale with their setting but the number of arrangements may overwhelm the room – in other words the proportion of arrangements to the room is not pleasing.

The idea of what makes pleasing proportions in flower arrangement changes with different generations. The early Chinese often placed a small branch and a single flower in a beautiful container and the latter was the most important. The Victorians used small posy-style arrangements on top of tall glass containers and were happy with them. At present it is considered that there should be a greater proportion of plant material to the other components in the design. In other words the plant material should dominate the

Pedestal Arrangements

This term refers to large designs placed on top of stands four feet, or more, high. The plant material should be larger in size for these designs than is normal, such as the largest hosta and bergenia leaves, big dahlias, tall delphiniums, peonies and hydrangeas.

Miniature Arrangements

These are the styles that are made in thimbles, dolls' house vases and other tiny containers. They are, in effect, reproductions of normal arrangements but use very much smaller plant material, such as the flowers of rock plants. Everything used in the design should be related in scale including the base, which is often inclined to dwarf the arrangement.

design. A guide line which has been evolved is that the plant material should be 1½ times the height or width of the container, whichever is the greatest measurement. The eye is a better guide, however, as so much depends on the type of container and its colour, pattern and texture and the colour and size of the plant material. For example, if the container is made of shiny coloured glass then the plant material, to look more important than the container, should probably be more than 1½ times the height of the container. If a heavy looking container – for example, a large bronze urn – is used with fine plant material such as pussy willow, then the plant material may need to be as much as 3 times the height of the container. Nature does not use equal amounts of things very often and there are many examples of a ratio of 2:3 or 3:5 being used – in other words about half as much again of one thing in proportion to the other. Landscape painters usually have more sea than sky or more sky than land and the horizon is seldom halfway across the canvas. Long narrow rooms and square ones are not as pleasing to sit in as rooms where two of the sides are just a little longer than the other two.

Equal amounts of things lack interest, conversely it is not pleasing to have one thing overwhelming the other. However, accurate measurement is unsuitable for flower arrangement and the eye is the best judge. A good test is to see, when the arrangement is completed, if the plant material looks more important than the container or if the eye goes first to the container. If it does the latter, then more plant material or something brighter or bolder is needed.

Practical Arrangements

Practise using good proportions in the following:
(A) A design using plant material the same height as the container. Then change to taller plant material and see which is more pleasing.
(B) An arrangement in a coloured glass container.
(C) A design using slender plant material and a heavy looking container and see which height of plant material is the more pleasing.
(D) A design using heavy, large plant material such as hydrangeas. Find the most pleasing height and one which does not overwhelm the container.

BALANCE

We do not enjoy any sense of unbalance in our environment – a tossing sea upsets us physically, a sloping floor feels uncomfortable, and we adjust a crooked picture on a wall. It makes no difference that we know the ship will not sink, the floor give way, or the picture fall down – we need the look of stability as well as the feel of it. We normally relate things to a horizontal line, such as a perfectly flat floor, and to a vertical line, such as the upright wall of a house.

In flower arrangement it is easy enough, once the mechanics are understood and have been practised, to see that the design actually stays upright and does not fall over. However, some designs still appear top-heavy, lopsided or bottom-heavy. This is referred to as visual balance.

In a lopsided arrangement something seems to be giving more visual weight to one side than the other or, to say it in another way, one's eyes are attracted more to one side than to the other. This means some things must have greater eye attraction or 'eye-pull' than others. It may be one white flower amongst other colours or an especially large flower amongst smaller ones. Certain objects do have greater eye-pull than others, all other qualities being equal.
1. Larger shapes attract the eye more quickly than smaller ones.
2. Brighter, more luminous and warmer colours are more eye-pulling than duller, less luminous and cooler colours.
3. Round shapes draw the eye sooner than lines and in-between shapes.
4. Shinier textures attract more than duller ones.
5. Denser, more compact forms are more eye-pulling than airier ones.

With this knowledge one can soon see the object that is causing the sense of unbalance and alter

Too much   Too little   Correct

Achieving correct proportions of plant material

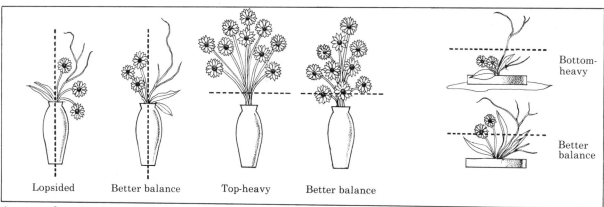

A sense of good balance is important in all designs

Lopsided   Better balance   Top-heavy   Better balance   Bottom-heavy   Better balance

it. To achieve a pleasing sense of balance the eyes need to be attracted equally to both sides of a design – that is either side of a central vertical axis. This does not mean that the objects themselves must be equal, which is monotonous, but a brilliant flower on one side of a container and a long branch on the other, though not equal in shape, colour, and size, can still attract equal attention.

Most people have a fair sense of balance and can feel any unbalance at once. If the reason for unbalance is not obvious, close the eyes and then rapidly open them and see which piece of plant material attracts the eye in the first place – it may be that this is too dominant in the design and its position needs altering, or it can be changed for something less dominant.

Another way of assessing balance is to hold a pencil up so that it appears to go through the centre of the container. This divides the two sides and it is easier to assess whether one side has more eye-pull than the other. If so, either remove some plant material from one side or add some to the other side.

Top-heaviness

Top-heaviness is sensed very quickly and often a container does actually fall over if there is too much plant material in it. This feeling can soon be corrected by reducing the amount of plant material or by transferring it to a larger container. Sometimes a top-heavy appearance is given by the design being too wide at the top and this is easily corrected by narrowing the top and widening the plant material nearer the container.

Bottom-heaviness

Bottom-heaviness is harder to recognise – probably because we quite enjoy a feeling of stability at the base of the design. However, if a base is too big in scale for the design, or if larger flowers are placed low down in the design, then it may have an appearance of bottom-heaviness, in which case the base should be reduced in size or the flowers should be lifted in the arrangement. The container may also be the cause of too much visual weight at the bottom of the design – it may have a shiny surface, strong colour or be too large for the plant material. In this case the plant material must be made more dominant by using a greater height or more brilliant colour.

Symmetry and Asymmetry

This refers to the outline of the shape of a design. If a design is symmetrical then its shape is exactly the same either side of the centre. Balance is easy to achieve in symmetrical designs as the shape is equal and therefore balanced. In asymmetrical designs the shapes are dissimilar and balance depends on the eye being equally attracted to both sides of the design. One reason for the popularity of triangular arrangements is that they are symmetrical and are easily balanced – they seem to 'sit well'. Within a symmetrical design it is not necessary for the plant material to be placed in exactly the same position on either side.

Balance by Placement

It is possible to achieve a sense of balance by altering the position of a flower arrangement on the table where it stands. The design on page 92 appears unbalanced, with all the plant material on one side of the container. If it is moved to the left of the table a better sense of balance is achieved. Usually a design is balanced for the centre of the container and this is placed in the centre of a table, but when all the plant material is placed on one side of the container, then the centre of the design does not coincide with the

90

The flowers of the iris are placed high in the design to balance the container

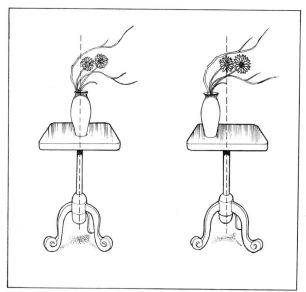

Achieving balance by placement

towards making a pleasing and harmonious whole.

It is perhaps easier to hear rhythm than to see it in a flower arrangement but the characteristics are the same – motion and rest in sequence. In flower arrangement your eyes should be able to travel easily round the whole design pausing occasionally and then moving on. The lines cause movement and the points create rest for the eyes. The rhythm of a design is poor if the eyes stop moving and cannot be taken from a large dominant flower (a bull's-eye), or by a lack of any lines along which to travel. Alternatively, too many lines and no resting places can give an uncomfortable, restless feeling to a design.

The secret of giving rhythm to a flower arrangement is found in the way it is achieved in other things – by repetition and easy, gradual change as in the dahlia petals. No definite formula can be given for flower arrangement and the rhythm is built up as the arrangement evolves, but the following suggestions are helpful.

centre of the container. A more pleasing sense of balance is obtained when the centre of the design, and not that of the container in this case, is placed in the centre of the table.

Practical Arrangements

Practise, to increase the sense of balance:
(A) A symmetrical arrangement.
(B) An asymmetrical arrangement.
(C) A design with the largest flowers at the top.
(D) A 'windswept' design, balanced by placement.

RHYTHM

Most of us are very conscious of the rhythm of music and our hands or feet may tap happily to it. The rhythm that we hear is determined by various notes and pauses and various sequences of notes and pauses, which are repeated and become part of a larger rhythmic pattern of sound. We recognise and enjoy this repetitive pattern.

Rhythm is a component part of life which is expressed in the repetitive cycles that occur throughout the world of nature. It can also be seen in the flight of birds and the swimming of fish and when people run or dance. Less actively there is rhythm in the lines left by the receding tide on a beach, in the branching of trees and in the petal formation of a dahlia. These radiate from a centre, being repeated and changing gradually in shape from the inside to the outside. Rhythm implies sequence and repetition, periods of movement and periods of rest, all contributing

Repetition

If basic shapes, or parts of shapes, are repeated, there is a sense of rhythm. For example, if curved plant material is used, combine it with a curved container and a round or oval base. If straight plant material is used, combine it with a straight-sided container and an angular base. The eyes find repetition and, therefore, a link in this way.

Including more than one of any type of plant material is also helpful. One of a kind usually stops the eye but two or more of a kind give a satisfying link, each has a 'friend' and the eye travels from one to another. For example, in a simple line arrangement lesser lines can support the main line just as small waves support the bigger ones.

When flowers are used in the line design, then two will give more rhythm than one. One of the flowers can be slightly smaller, or less far open, to give variety and can be placed at a slightly different angle.

It is helpful to repeat colours as well as shapes. If there is only one splash of a colour and no link anywhere else in the design, then the eyes continually travel to this single colour and there is no repetition to move the eye along.

Transition

This is not an easy word but it means gradual change. A tree trunk is broad and then it gradually gets thinner and leads into smaller branches finally tapering into slender twigs. This is a good example of transition. The eyes travel easily along without startling change. Stems of delphinium and lupin show this gradual change also. In traditional arrangements especially, smaller flowers are used at the extremities of the design, and then flowers which are a little larger towards the centre, with the largest at the centre. The more in-between sizes there are in the design, the more gentle the rhythm.

Transitional shapes between lines and points help the rhythm of the design. Using more space on the outside of the design and a density of plant material in the centre also gives rhythm. Colour may be gentler if there is a stepping stone between colours that are not very close, for example, if orange is used between red and yellow to act as a link. Transition gives an easy rhythm but this is not the only kind of rhythm and a stronger more exciting rhythm results from using less transition and sharper contrasts.

Simplicity

A jumble of plant material has little rhythm – flowers and leaves overlap, branches go in all directions and there are no 'paths' to follow. Trimming lines and removing unwanted foliage gives more clarity and therefore more rhythm, as the eyes see definite paths. Sometimes it seems hard to remove plant material but it usually gives a better design. Too much overlapping foliage and many small buds are distracting and superfluous to the design. Modern designs using little plant material look sleeker and more rhythmic if only three varieties of plant material are used – one for the points, one for the lines, and another for the in-between shapes.

Radiation

There are many examples of radiation in nature. This means starting all lines from a given point and it gives a satisfying sense of order and rhythm. It is seen in a palm leaf, a dahlia flower, a rosette of echeveria leaves, a yucca plant. It is also seen in a winter tree as the branches divide in all directions from the central trunk. It is a delightful way to compose a flower arrangement. The stem ends are put near together on the pinholder and then the stems radiate outwards in all directions, giving a greater effect of elegance. It is not essential for a design to radiate and very modern designs do not often radiate from a central point but it is very suitable for traditional arrangements. It is also a convenient type of construction for flower arrangers as all the stem ends can be centred in one place in the container.

Rhythm given by the repetition of curves in the plant material – whitebeam and camellias – the handle of the pewter container and the legs of the trivet

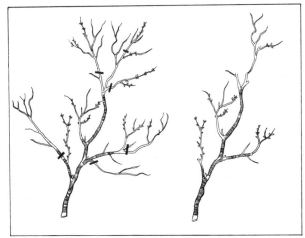

Removing unwanted foliage and branches

The petals of a dahlia flower illustrate the qualities of rhythm, transition and radiation

Curved Plant Material

This is usually considered more rhythmic than straight plant material, probably because the curves may be repeated in one branch.

Creating an Atmosphere through Rhythm

Rhythm is very expressive and an atmosphere can be created through the type of rhythm used. When there is much transition a gentle feeling is present. When there are more contrasts and spaces the design is more active. Curved plant material can give a playful atmosphere and a dancing feeling and straight rhythmic lines can give a strong, rigid appearance.

Practical Arrangements

To practise various types of rhythm:
(A) A design of all bare branches, pruning them to give rhythm.
(B) A fan-shaped design of straight lines radiating from a centre.
(C) A design interpreting 'March winds' or 'a tornado'.
(D) A design interpreting elegance with a gentle rhythm using plenty of transitional plant material.
(E) A design interpreting a piece of music or a dance.

EMPHASIS

A good design makes some of its parts more important than others. Most successful theatrical productions have in their casts star performers and also smaller part actors, and a play or ballet in which all the roles are equally significant seems dull and lacking in cohesion. In good paintings there are areas which have more interest than other areas and a story usually has a few dominant characters and other lesser ones. A garden often features one or two specimen trees which appear more important than the other plants.

When all the parts of any design are of equal attraction they tend to compete for attention and the result is a lack of unity. A sense of order can be more easily achieved when there are a few dominant qualities in the design and the remainder is subordinated.

A flower arrangement consists of many things assembled together: a container and often a base, sometimes one or more accessories and a drape or background, and, of course, varying numbers of flowers, leaves and other plant material. To create a good flower arrangement, something in this group of objects needs to be emphasised and made more important. Most flower arrangers of this generation agree that it should be the plant material, with everything else subordinated and used to create a setting and give support. Within the grouping of plant material there should also be a dominant quality. Beautiful flowers always attract attention and it is easy for them to become the 'star performers in the production' of a flower arrangement. However, it is tiring when there are only star performers and there is nothing else to look at. We cannot maintain heightened interest indefinitely and so a period of less concentration is necessary, meaning something less eye-catching at which to look. Plain leaves, smaller flowers, the container and base can all give variety to an arrangement without competing strongly with the main attraction of the flowers.

It is interesting to test your eyes when looking at a flower arrangement – they usually go quickly to the larger flowers and then, tiring a little, pass on to the other parts of the design with less concentrated attention. Eventually, after these travels, they return once more to the beautiful and dominant flowers.

Creating Emphasis

Larger flowers. There are various ways of making something more important but the easiest is to use a few flowers which are larger than all the others. Larger objects always attract the eye before smaller ones, and so seem more important.

Points. These are usually more compelling shapes than others and cause the eye to rest for a while on them. This makes them seem dominant in a design.

Brighter colours. Colours which are brighter or more luminous in an arrangement tend to attract the eyes more quickly than other colours and so give emphasis.

Shiny textures. These are more eye-attracting and can help to make plant material more predominant than duller surfaces. It follows that plant material that is larger than the rest, is a rounded shape, has bright or luminous colouring and a shiny texture can easily become dominant in an arrangement and may be used to give emphasis.

Too Much Emphasis

It is possible to over-emphasise something in the design. For example, two large orange dahlias may be used for emphasis, but when placed in position they could appear as bull's-eyes, from which you cannot take your eyes and which soon give an uncomfortable feeling. In this case it is better to use smaller flowers or some of a duller colour to restore a pleasing balance of importance and unimportance to the design.

Competition

When the base, container, drape or accessory is very large or has brilliant colour or shiny texture, the result is strong competition for the plant material. To correct this the plant material must be especially striking to offset the counter-attractions. It may be safer to use the duller colours and textures for the components which are normally subordinated.

Plant Material other than Flowers

Sometimes the initial inspiration for an arrangement may be a beautiful piece of driftwood. Any other plant material should then be played down and only a small grouping of flowers and foliage (if any) should be used if the wood is to remain the dominant and inspiring feature.

It is difficult to create emphasis in an all-foliage arrangement as there are few leaves in the point shape. More brilliant colouring is helpful if it is used in the centre and rosettes of leaves can be made to give an impression of a point.

Position in the Design

Where should the dominant feature be placed in a design? There are no rules for this, but in traditional designs a few larger flowers are usually placed in the centre, with all other stems radiating from them. The terms used to describe this emphasised area are 'centre of interest' or 'focal point'.

In the more modern designs the dominant plant material may be placed *anywhere* in the design and there may be more than one position for it. The only concern is that the balance is not upset, as can so easily happen if one very dominant flower is placed on one side without anything equally attracting elsewhere. The term used for the dominant areas in a modern design is often 'the emphasis points'.

Practical Arrangements

To practise emphasising a part of the design:
(A) A traditional arrangement without any large flowers, and then with two larger flowers placed in the centre.
(B) An arrangement of all line plant material, and then add two points.
(C) An arrangement of foliage and create a centre of interest with a rosette of leaves of a brighter colour than the rest.
(D) A modern design placing two rounded flowers at the top of the arrangement.

CONTRAST

Contrast and variety are a vital part of our lives and we need the interest they provide. How quickly the fashions change in clothes and each

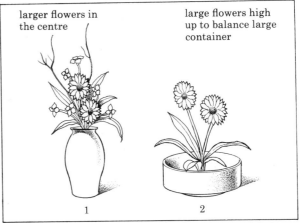

Different positions for the dominant material in a design. 1. Traditional 2. Modern

new style seems quite different from the styles of a year or two earlier. We do our daily jobs for a certain period of time then we need a change and a holiday. Contrast and variety add the spice to life and opposite things emphasise and intensify each other, often one being unknown without the other, such as city and countryside, darkness and light, gaiety and depression, beauty and ugliness.

If you have lived in a country without any perceptible change in the seasons you will remember missing the contrast between the warmth of the hot season and the chill of a cold one. The first flower of spring in Britain – the snowdrop – seems infinitely more precious after a season without flowers. The Chinese have an old saying that 'The harmonious balance of opposites is the underlying principle of the universe'.

A flower arrangement can be dull without contrasts or, at least, some variation to give interest and avoid monotony. A brilliant flower looks more exciting when placed near a plain green leaf just as a simple dress offsets a pretty hat. Too many things of equal interest are dull and a simple dress worn with a plain hat may lack excitement and seem uninteresting in the same way that a pretty hat with an equally pretty dress may lack the value of contrast.

Creating Contrast in Shape

An arrangement of all rounded forms can be uninteresting and to give variety some should be turned to face different ways. To provide more contrast line plant material and in-between shapes may also be used.

Texture

As this is not a dominant quality, very strong contrasts in texture may be used to give interest as similar textures can be monotonous.

Colour

This is such a vital and compelling quality that strong contrasts may seem too exciting for the eye and a slight variation in the colours used may be all that is necessary for interest.

Use of Contrast

Traditional designs depend on *variations* of colour, shape and texture rather than strong contrasts and the interest lies in a mass of many colours, textures and shapes. More modern designs, which use less plant material, depend on strong *contrasts* for providing the interest and for emphasising the special qualities apparent in the plant material.

Too Much Contrast

Contrasts can sometimes upset unity, especially when there is no link between the two opposite things. This does not often happen with one arrangement but it does occur when two arrangements are placed near to each other – perhaps in a niche at a show. Co-ordination is difficult unless the two designs contain some things which are related – perhaps similar colours, containers or plant material.

Practical Arrangements

Practise using contrast and variation:

(A) A modern design using very different shapes and textures.
(B) A modern arrangement using contrasts in colour.
(C) A traditional arrangement using variations in the colouring and shapes.
(D) Interpret drama, heat and cold, sun and moon, spring and autumn.

HARMONY

This word is beautiful both in sound and meaning. When people live peacefully together they live in harmony. The sounds and silences of music can be combined to give beautiful harmony. A tree has many parts – roots, trunk, branches, bark and leaves which are all individually beautiful but also contribute to a harmonious whole. In a pleasing flower arrangement the plant material, container, base, accessory and setting are all in harmony. Harmony, then, infers agreement between people or things brought together as one.

Why is it that some things seem to look agreeable together and others appear out of place? It is usually because some relationship can be seen between objects that look right together – it may be colours, shapes, association or a common habitat – there is some link which relates them. This is usually easier to recognise and enjoy than to create in a design. However, it soon becomes second nature to look carefully at plant material and the other components of flower arrangement, knowing that you are trying to find relationships between them.

A pedestal arrangement using large flowers – lilies, delphiniums and hydrangea – all in scale with the setting

Rhythm seen in the transition of trunk to twigs in a winter tree

Appearance

There are similarities between materials in their outward appearance. These 'echoes' give repetition and so a feeling of agreement. For example, the colour of the container may be a darker version of the colour of some of the flowers and this provides a link; the curve of a piece of driftwood may repeat the curve of a figurine; texture may be repeated with a velvet-covered base and the velvet texture of a pansy in the arrangement. The resemblance need not be exactly similar but a link in appearance, however small, is an echo giving a feeling of pleasing relationship.

Association

People are quick to associate objects with places, ideas or other objects. For example, it is easy to see a relationship between a group of things collected while beachcombing – shells, sand, sea holly, grasses, driftwood, feathers – all from the same habitat and therefore giving a sense of harmony. Alternatively, another group of objects may remind us of another country or a hot climate. Rich dark colours (especially violet), chenille fabric, ornate vases, lace mats and ferns are associated, by many people, with the Victorian age and there is a sense of agreement when they are used together. The use of only one component which is never associated with the Victorian period – for example a perspex base – can ruin the effect completely and give disharmony.

Flower arrangers must be squirrels hoarding all kinds of things which might just provide the right link in a design – hunting down the right components is all part of the fun! A flower arrangement is rather like a jigsaw puzzle – there are many pieces but each one must fit or the puzzle will not present a complete picture when it is finished.

Styles

It is easy to create any styles once the principles of design are understood, for they are the basis for all types of flower arrangement, both old and new. However, it is impossible to think of all these design principles as you work – this is inhibiting and it is better to create an arrangement spontaneously. Very soon using the design principles well becomes second nature and an experienced flower arranger can pinpoint faults quickly, such as 'there is no feeling of rhythm' or 'the flowers and leaves are not in scale' or 'there is a lack of contrast'. It is helpful to study flower arrangements at shows and in books and magazines, and to look at their good and bad use of design principles. After creating an arrangement try assessing its design. It is better not to make any alterations unless they are very simple. When another arrangement is made, the previous fault will be remembered and corrected. In assessing whether you have used the design principles well, ask yourself these questions:

1. Is everything related in size? (scale)
2. Is there too much plant material for the container? (proportion)
3. Is the design lopsided, bottom-heavy or top-heavy? (balance)
4. Do my eyes travel easily around the design? (rhythm)
5. Do my eyes stop and rest at some things which are more dominant than the others? (emphasis)
6. Are there contrasts or variety in shapes, textures and colours? (contrast)

STYLES

There are many styles in flower arrangement in the same way that there are many styles in painting, sculpture, furniture and so on. Some are classical and others are new and controversial but all give variety and interest to the art of flower arrangement. New styles are essential to the activity of any art and inevitable because of our ever-changing world.

Styles alter for various reasons: a scientific discovery may give a new material – this happened in flower arrangement when the arrival of plastic foam made new shapes possible; social conditions have an influence also, for example, life in Victorian Britain encouraged elaborate and formal table arrangements; a greater production and exchange of books between countries gives new ideas; faster transport brings interesting plant materials from abroad. It is also true to say that trends in one art usually influence styles in others and this is the reason for the present interest in abstract styles of flower arrangement.

Styles are easier to recognise in retrospect because a general trend is not immediately obvious. New styles may be so well accepted that they become firm classics while others have only a short life after being tried and considered. In flower arrangement broad classifications are recognised, although there are many variations within them. There are also hybrids which may fit into more than one group.

It is always stimulating to try different ways of arranging plant material instead of getting into the rut of one style. It is also exciting to try entirely new styles as all artists should experiment to find out the limitations and possibilities of their materials. This is the only way that an art can progress.

The following are the main classifications:

TRADITIONAL STYLE

In Britain this term refers to the style of flower arrangement created from Edwardian times to the Second World War. Another term that might be used to describe it is classical and it is always well loved and practised. This style originated in the large country houses and cottages from arrangements using garden plant material. It began by being somewhat shapeless but it contained many beautiful varieties of plant material arranged with a flowing effect.

The term traditional now applies also to the more ordered mass arrangements which gradually developed and which are often in the shape of a

Above: A Christmas arrangement in crescent shape of variegated holly, roses, skimmia berries and Christmas roses in a Georgian candelabra

Opposite: 'In the manner of a Flemish flower painting.' The flowers, container, fruit and bird's nest reflect the mood of the adjacent painting

"The Gardener's Shed."
Baxter Print.

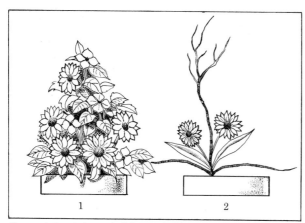

Geometric styles   1. Mass   2. Line

fabric and sometimes covered boards or trays are used (page 15).

GEOMETRIC STYLE

As interest in flower arrangement increased after the Second World War there came a desire to experiment with different styles. At the same time the environment in which people lived was becoming more streamlined and inevitably this showed up in flower arrangements, as in other forms of art. In trying new ways with plant material it was found that recognisable geometric shapes could be formed so that the outline, or silhouette, conformed to a crescent, a triangle, a diagonal, a circle, a vertical (an arrangement with strong vertical movement), a Hogarth curve or 'S' shape (so called because William Hogarth considered this the most beautiful line), and so on. At first these shapes appeared rather stiff and contrived but they have become softer and less rigid over the years.

These styles can be made with a lot of plant material or a little, in other words with a mass or a line appearance.

Plant material. Generally fewer varieties are used than in the traditional style to give a more ordered effect. The curved shapes such as crescents and Hogarth curves need curvilinear plant material and verticals, diagonals and triangles need straighter growing plant material.

Containers. A Hogarth curve and a diagonal need a taller container so that the lower curves or lines may be seen. The other shapes can be made in any type of container.

Supports. It is easier to position the stems with accuracy in plastic foam. When creating a Hogarth curve or a diagonal the lower curving stems are almost impossible to place at the correct angle if wire netting or a pinholder are used. Much depends on the amount of plant material in the design; plastic foam needs more plant material to conceal it than a pinholder and the clarity of the shape may be lost when many leaves are added to cover the mechanics. A pinholder is the best support when a small quantity of plant material is used.

Design. Larger rounded flowers giving a clear centre of interest are normally used in the centre of the design, as in the traditional style, with smaller plant material at the extremities. It is very important to watch the spaces around the outline so that the geometric shape is clear. First placements of plant material usually set the shape of the arrangement.

triangle, circle or oval. The chief characteristics of any traditional arrangement are a mass of plant material, with often a closely related colour scheme, and emphasis on the outline of the mass rather than on individual plant materials. Little space is used within the design itself. It is a favourite style, as it is highly decorative, for cathedrals and churches (especially for weddings) and for large social occasions and events. It can be of any size and anything from miniatures to massive pedestal arrangements can be termed traditional.

Plant material. A large amount of varied plant material is used with variety in texture and shape.

Containers. The original traditional designs used deep urns which hold a lot of water for the numerous stems. Nowadays, arrangements in this style use containers which are traditional in appearance but the present-day supports for stems have made it possible to use a variety of more unusual containers such as candlesticks, candelabras and baskets. Pedestals are often used, either as part of the container or as a separate stand.

Supports. Glass roses and moss were used in early days but now wire netting and plastic foam are usual, often combined with a pinholder. It must be remembered that a lot of water is necessary for these traditional arrangements as there are many stems taking up water from the container or plastic foam.

Design. A description of how to make a traditional triangular design is described on page 34. When making an oval or circular arrangement it is often easier to start at the side and not the centre of the design.

Bases. Early traditional designs did not include bases unless they were part of the container or were a separate antique stand on which the container normally stood. Present-day bases for traditional arrangements are often of draped

102

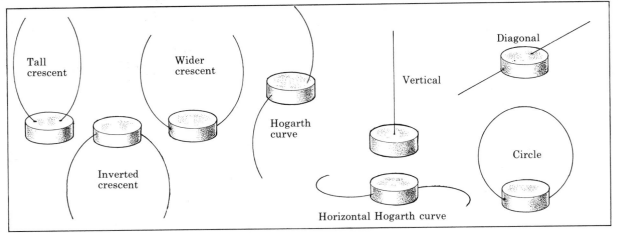

First placements of plant material set the shape of the arrangement

A Hogarth Curve

COMPONENTS

(A) A stemmed container such as a candlestick or a figurine, with a candlecup mounted on the top. This lifts the arrangement and enables the lower curve to be seen clearly.
(B) Plastic foam, with a foam pinholder if desired.
(C) Wire netting to cover the foam (as a cap) with reel wire to secure it.
(D) Curved plant material such as branches, broom, driftwood, blossom. A Hogarth curve cannot be designed with straight stems.
(E) Several rounded flowers larger than the others.
(F) Some plain, oval or rounded leaves.
(G) Some smaller flowers and foliage to fill in.

METHOD

Make sure the plastic foam stands *above* the rim of the container. Place a tall, curved piece of plant material in a vertical position on the top of the plastic foam but to one side, with the tip curving inwards. Place a second piece of plant material (it need not be the same variety) in the side of the plastic foam on the opposite side, bending downwards and with the tip also turning inwards. This gives an 'S' shape. Try to keep to this shape by placing all the other plant material so that it follows these lines. Other lesser pieces may be added to support the first placements and give greater visual weight.

Several of the largest flowers should be placed in the centre, usually with only one of them facing full on, the others being slightly turned. Add leaves and smaller flowers following the line of the curves. Some plain leaves with short stems can be placed around the central flowers to hide the plastic foam and provide a framework for the flowers. Watch the spaces around the curves to avoid losing the shape. When you have finished make sure the mechanics do not show.

Crescent

COMPONENTS

(A) Any container.
(B) Plastic foam (with a foam pinholder if desired) for a mass design or a pinholder for a line design.
(C) Curved plant material as for the Hogarth curve.
(D) Some larger rounded flowers (or points).
(E) A few plain leaves.
(F) Some smaller flowers and leaves to fill in.

METHOD

Place a curved stem at one side of the foam and then a second stem on the other side to complete the crescent shape. Add a few larger flowers at the centre and fill in with transitional plant material as with the Hogarth curve. Make sure the mechanics do not show. The crescent may be placed in various ways in a container.

The crescent with curves turning downwards needs a stemmed or tall container. The horizontal type looks better in a low container so that it can be seen from above.

Vertical

This term refers to a design with a strong vertical movement. It may be a slim triangle or a rectangle, but it is very tall for its width.

COMPONENTS

(A) Any container but preferably not a wide one.
(B) Pinholder or plastic foam (a foam pinholder if desired).
(C) Wire netting, with reel wire to secure it if necessary.
(D) Some tall straight growing plant material such as iris leaves, bulrushes or gladioli.
(E) Some round or oval leaves to cover the pinholder or some other 'cover-up' for the mechanics,

Above: A free-form arrangement of strelitzia in a Maltese glass container
Opposite: The Madonna Lily with hosta leaves arranged in a design with vertical movement

A diagonal arrangement of tulips, willow catkins and foliage in a carved wooden box. As the container is not waterproof, the mechanics consist of plastic foam enclosed in a polythene bag

such as a small piece of driftwood or a stone.
(F) A few rounded flowers larger than the others.
(G) A few leaves and smaller flowers.

METHOD
Place the tall stems in the container. Add the larger, rounded flowers keeping them towards the centre and following the vertical line. Cover the mechanics and add smaller flowers and leaves if desired.

Diagonal

COMPONENTS
(A) Container.
(B) Plastic foam with wire netting and a foam pinholder if desired.
(C) Straight growing plant material.
(D) A few rounded flowers larger than the rest.
(E) Some smaller flowers and some in-between shapes in leaves.

METHOD
Make sure the plastic foam stands above the rim of the container. Place the tallest piece of plant material into the top of the plastic foam and to one side in a slanting position. Add another shorter, straight piece of plant material into the other side of the plastic foam low down and slanting to give the effect of forming a straight line with the first piece. Add larger flowers at the centre and smaller flowers and foliage as stepping stones.

Circular and triangular designs have been described in the third chapter.

Bases

These may be added to any of the geometric styles depending on the visual weight of the arrangement and the container. If the arrangement seems big for the container, then a base may correct this. If the container seems big for the plant material do *not* add a base as this makes the plant material seem even smaller in comparison to the container.

Geometric designs were new in the Fifties, but they now tend to appear as classical designs as other styles have evolved.

FREE-FORM

For a while all varieties of plant material were arranged with a definite and recognisable geometric outline, but trial and error proved that some were not suitable. For example, bulrushes with their rigid stems are impossible to arrange in a Hogarth curve. Some branches or driftwood of great beauty do not appear to conform to any geometric shape except by a wide stretch of the imagination. It was also realised that it can be unnecessarily restricting to conform always to a set shape. Nowadays the geometric style is often used but other designs have developed which are more suitable for some plant material. A new style is usually a complete change from the one immediately before and so 'free-form', meaning free of geometric form, was the term given to the new style. It refers to designs without a definite geometric outline in which there is usually a lot of space so that the individual beauty of each piece of plant material is emphasised instead of the beauty of an outline shape and a mass of plant material.

Plant material. Bold plant material of distinctive quality is used with restraint. It is often strongly contrasting and dramatic. Many free-form designs use one type of plant material for the lines, one for the points and one for the in-between shapes.

Containers. Modern containers such as stoneware, hand-made pottery and glass are more usual and the shapes are simple with interesting textures.

Supports. As free-form designs are restrained in the use of plant material, plastic foam is often not suitable since it is more difficult to conceal. A pinholder is soon hidden and it is not necessary to do this only with plant material. Stones, windscreen glass, driftwood and so on can effectively cover the mechanics without cluttering up the design with unnecessary plant material.

Design. Space is considered as much as the plant material in the design and each piece is clearly seen so that the curve of a piece of driftwood, the shape of a flower and a lovely texture can be enjoyed. The natural growth of the plant material is usually followed. In theory there could be mass designs which are free of geometric form but in practice they can appear shapeless and unattractive; so free-form usually refers to designs using more space and tending to be linear in effect.

The main difference between traditional and geometric designs and the free-form style is in the type of balance. The former depend on the shape of the arrangement for balance. In free-form, balance is dependent on assembling plant material with equal eye-pull on either side of the design. For example, a long branch on one side may balance a brilliant flower on the other.

The arrangement described on page 28 is a simple free-form design. The method of assembling is further described so that you may use any plant material.

COMPONENTS

(A) A modern container.
(B) Pinholder.
(c) A 'cover-up' for the mechanics.
(D) Plant material in scale with the container. It is

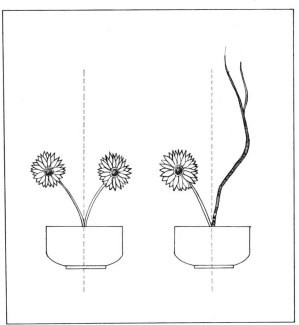

Left: Balance obtained with similar shapes. *Right:* Balance with dissimilar shapes

suggested that a start is made with one variety of plant material for lines, one for points and one for an in-between shape.

METHOD

Place a piece of plant material on one side of the container. This unbalances the container, giving a lopsided effect. Now add a different piece of plant material to the other side so that the design appears more balanced. Look at the arrangement to see to which side your eyes are drawn the least. Add some more plant material to this side, it may be the same as before or something different.

Continue with this balancing and unbalancing routine alternately, until you feel that there is enough plant material in the design. Any plant material placed in the centre does not affect the balance. Make sure the design appears balanced before you finish.

LANDSCAPE

This is a very charming style and more realistic than any other because it is similar to a small part of a lakeside, garden, woodland, seashore, stream, mountain or moor. It is not difficult because it is a copy of a natural scene and only good observation is necessary, such as seeing the way in which moss grows over a stone, feathers peep out of sand, trees bend with the wind and so on.

The secret of an effective landscape design is to use restraint. The natural scene may be a little

107

Above: The blue poppy, *Meconopsis grandis*, and hosta leaves arranged simply to show their beauty
Opposite: This triangular arrangement of common wild flowers includes ragwort, Lady's Bedstraw and fennel

Assembling a modern design: 1. A piece of driftwood is placed to the left of the container

2. To balance the arrangement a glycerined leaf is added to the right of the container

untidy but the landscape design could produce the same atmosphere with a more ordered effect. There may be pebbles all over the bed of a lake but in a container this could look unattractive and two or three pebbles should be enough to suggest the lake scene. The viewer's imagination can carry this suggestion further. Similarly, a base completely covered with moss or sand can look very heavy and untidy whereas less of each can still convey the right atmosphere.

It is also important to avoid man-made objects which would normally not be present in the portrayed scene. China animals may not look natural enough, a formal container would not be seen and a flat painted background of a sky can give a more natural effect than draped fabric.

Plant material. This should be in keeping with the scene portrayed. A woodland could use driftwood, ferns and moss and, if the design is for a flower arrangement show, the plant material should be of a variety which naturally grows in the habitat shown. For example, an outdoor fern should be used and not a fern from a greenhouse, although there is nothing to stop you using the latter to give the atmosphere when arranging for your home.

Containers. It is normal to use a hidden container in this style although a low one may be used to give the effect of a lake when making a 'water' arrangement. (This term refers to arrangements in which water is featured and not only used to supply the stem ends with moisture.)

Bases. A crosscut of unpolished wood or a piece of slate or stone give a more natural appearance for a landscape design than a man-made base.

Supports. Plastic foam or a pinholder may be

used but the latter is easier to conceal. Stones, which would naturally appear in the scene portrayed, make good cover-ups.

Design. The arrangement should appear realistic, with the plant material being used exactly as it grows.

Practical Arrangements

Practise a landscape design by collecting materials during a walk and then assembling them at home on a wooden base or a piece of slate. Driftwood, shells, sand, sea holly and feathers may be picked up while beachcombing. Leaves, wood, moss, branches, ferns and pine cones may be found in a wood. Heather, stones and wood may be collected on a mountainside.

PERIOD

When traditional and present-day arrangements have been practised it is interesting to see how flowers were arranged long ago, because flower arrangement is as old as civilisation. We know that flowers have been placed in containers of water since about 2800 BC and that they have also been used for ceremonies and festivities all through history, sometimes decoratively and sometimes symbolically. Whenever there has been a stable and settled civilisation with people living harmoniously together, there have been flower arrangements of some kind, even though periodically there have been dark ages when no arts developed or were enjoyed. The study of period design is fascinating and broadens the whole

3. The design is once more unbalanced by the addition of pieces of coral

4. Two hippeastrum flowers are added towards the right of the container and complete the design

field of flower arrangement. It is interesting to see one's own arrangements in the context of history and many ideas can also be gained for the present day.

Each period has a distinctive style which reflects the social conditions and environment of the times. The Egyptians, for example, liked simplicity, repetition and regularity in all their art and their arrangements, often of the sacred lotus flower, showed these trends. The people who lived in Holland in the 17th and 18th Centuries were quite fascinated with plants of all kinds and horticulture reached new heights. As a result the paintings of the Dutch and Flemish Old Masters show many varieties of flowers arranged in a loving manner. The rather rigid social structure in Victorian times is reflected in their formal designs often using stiff, wired stems.

Any arrangement made now, in a style of a period in the past, can only be made 'in the manner' of former times, as it is not always possible to find authentic containers and many of the varieties of plant material are no longer in existence. However, it is certainly possible to reproduce the spirit and atmosphere of earlier flower arrangements. Unfortunately, there are no photographs to study but there are other sources which can provide information. In addition to literature, there are paintings, tapestries, wood carvings, mosaics, coins, rugs, illuminated manuscripts, furniture and engravings which illustrate period flower arrangements. These may be seen in stately homes, museums and art galleries all over the world. If you have the opportunity to see any, look carefully at the following:

1. The shape and material of the container.

A landscape design using blackthorn, moss and primroses with a bird and a stone as accessories

This pot-et-fleur includes a range of foliage plants – ricinus, kentia, peperomia, maranta and ferns. The flowering plants can be added in the spring

A Victorian washbowl makes an ideal container for a pot-et-fleur. The plants are arranged in the compost without their pots and flowers may be added in the centre if desired

2. The shape of the flower arrangement.
3. The varieties of plant material.
4. The colours of the flowers and the surroundings.
5. The position in which flowers were placed in a room.
6. The type of base, if one was used.
7. Accessories or associated objects.
8. The purpose of the arrangement.
9. The style of the furnishings and architecture.
10. The spirit or manner of the flower arrangement.

Consider also if any ideas could be adapted for present-day arrangements.

POT-ET-FLEUR

This is a decoration, or style, which uses cut flowers combined with growing plants, which may be in or out of their own pots. This is a most useful style for winter when flowers are scarce or expensive as it uses very few. It is also a good way to grow plants, which often thrive when placed near each other, and for centrally heated homes it is an excellent form of long-lasting decoration.

Container. This must be deep enough to hold plenty of compost for the roots of plants. In the case of plants used in their own pots it must be large enough to hold the pots. It must also be possible to water the plants easily without spilling water on to the furniture. Victorian wash bowls are excellent and so are old saucepans and cooking pots, soup and vegetable tureens, big bowls and tubs.

Plant material. The plants must all need approximately the same amount of water, temperature, light and humidity if they are to thrive. For example, a cactus needs very little water and will soon die if grown in the same compost as a hydrangea which needs a lot of water. The cut flowers may be of any variety which suits the design.

Supports. The plants are supported by their own roots and stems in the compost or by their own pots. The cut flowers are best supported by a pinholder in a tin (or a well-type) placed in the

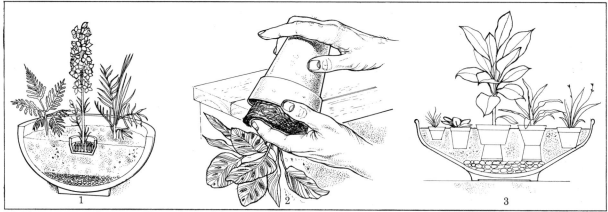

Making a pot-et-fleur 1. Plants in position together with a well pinholder to hold fresh flowers 2. Knocking a plant from its pot before placing it in the arrangement 3. A design with plants left in their pots

compost. Single flowers may be placed into small tubes, or cigar cases, and strapped with sticky tape to strong stems or plunged into the compost.

Design. The same considerations are necessary in design as for all other styles and there should be a good use of the basic design principles. As the plants may tend to look rather similar, strong contrasts in form and texture are effective. The flowers can add sparkle with their colours, but a variety of greens may be used in the plants. It is also possible to use grey, brown and red leaved plants. Good height is normally necessary to balance the large container needed for the roots or pots.

A Pot-et-fleur without Individual Pots

COMPONENTS
(A) A bag of John Innes No. 2 Compost.
(B) Gravel.
(C) Charcoal.
(D) Large container.
(E) A number of plants which need the same conditions in which to grow and give a variety of shape, texture and colour.
(F) Cut flowers.
(G) Container and pinholder for the flowers.

METHOD
1. Place about one inch of washed gravel on the bottom of the container for good drainage. Sprinkle broken-up charcoal over this to keep the water sweet. Add John Innes Compost on the top to a depth of about two inches. Remove the plants from their pots by turning them upside down and rapping the edge of the pot against something hard. The plant should drop into the hand easily (watering before doing this is not advisable).
2. Place the plants, complete with their root balls, on top of the compost and arrange them as desired.

When you are happy with the design, fill the spaces between the plants with more compost and firm in the plants. There should be no compost in the top one inch of the container to leave room for watering. Plants may be positioned at an angle and it is not necessary for them all to be placed upright.
3. Add a well-type pinholder for the flowers and press it gently into the compost. Place cut flowers amongst the plants when desired.

The pot-et-fleur should be looked after in the same way that each plant should be cared for if it were left in its own pot. It is probable that less water will be needed as the larger container does not dry out as quickly.
4. Stones, driftwood, shells and other similar objects may be added to provide interest.

A Pot-et-fleur with Plants left in their Pots

A very large container or trough will be needed. Stand the individual pots on gravel, sprinkled with charcoal in the same way as before, and then fill the spaces with moist peat in place of compost. This gives a bulky design and it is not always easy to add flowers amongst the pots.

ABSTRACT DESIGNS

The influences of the 20th Century have led to abstract art which is very different from the representational art of the past. Flower arrangement has always been more abstract than representational, as flowers arranged in a container do not look exactly as they do when growing in a garden. The only form of representational design in flower arrangement is a landscape which is a true copy of a natural scene. So when we speak of 'abstract' designs in flower arrangement we mean

114

those that look more unrealistic than others, and are at the opposite end of the scale from the landscape style. The further the design departs from using plant material in a naturalistic manner the more abstract it becomes.

It is wise not to try abstract designs until the skill of supporting plant material is fully understood, because the mechanics can be a challenge. The reason is that little plant material is used and the mechanics can be far more visible and difficult to conceal. Also stem ends are not necessarily centred in a container of water and, therefore, the methods of support are more complicated.

Two styles have developed in abstract flower arrangement – decorative and expressive. Decorative makes *patterns* with plant material using flowers, leaves and stems for shape, colour and texture, without regard for the way the plant grows. This is a form of abstract which has no subject matter or meaning and is meant to be enjoyed for its design qualities only.

John Piper's wonderful stained glass windows in Coventry Cathedral present the beauty of colour in its own right without linking it to figures and 'a story' as do the more traditional stained glass windows. A decorative abstract design using plant material asks you to enjoy the organisation of space, shapes, colours and textures without looking for a meaning. Many traditional forms of decorative flower arrangement also do this, but with the abstract style the outward look has a far stronger sense of design, and there are no unnecessary details. Much more space is used within the design.

The other style of abstract which has developed in flower arrangement, *expressive*, uses plant material symbolically to interpret a subject. There is a message which the flower arranger conveys to the viewer through the medium of plant material. Sometimes these two styles are called non-objective (decorative) and objective (expressive). The latter is easier to do because it does not make patterns as in the decorative style. Plant material is not easy to manipulate into patterns because of its fragility. Needlework thread, clay, paint and so on are very much easier for the artist to alter and form into new images than plant material.

Decorative Abstract

Plant material. There should be definite design qualities present in the plant material – this may be a clear shape, exciting texture or strong colour. In other words plant material that has strong

A decorative abstract design

'personality' and is not indeterminate in shape, texture or colour. Patterns are made more easily with definite shapes, such as long leaves and stems, and round flowers. The plant material may be used unchanged or it can be twisted, tied, bent or cut to achieve the desired pattern. It is often necessary to 'play' with the plant material to see what can be made with it before starting a design. Preserved plant materials may be easier to use as they avoid the need for a container of water, which can be limiting.

Containers. Containers should be very modern in appearance and some of the new materials, such as perspex, can be used. The container, if unconcealed, is very much a part of the design and not merely a receptacle for water. It should be considered as an integral part of the complete arrangement. A container with more than one opening is useful in creating an abstract as it helps to avoid radiation which, if used, may give a natural rather than an abstract effect.

Supports. A pinholder is usually a more suitable support as it can be easily concealed. If it is cleaned or painted it may even be shown as part of the design. Black stones can be used to cover it successfully as they are not noticeable in the design. When water is not necessary, Plasticine, plaster of Paris and other similar materials can hold stems in place and in many positions.

Design. When creating an abstract, think of the

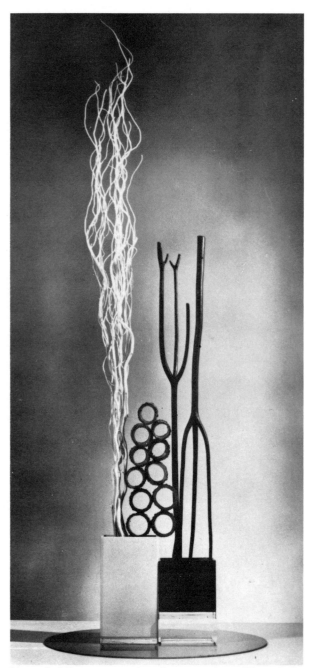

'Apartheid'. An expressive abstract using willow, drift-wood and hogweed with perspex containers and base

give a naturalistic appearance like a tree growing from a central trunk. As in all designing, the principles of design should be the basis and plant material should predominate.

Practical Arrangements

Practise making a design with only one type of plant material, such as straight stems, and forming them, by bending, into a pattern enclosing interesting spaces. Then try a design based on a circle with everything emphasising the circular shape. Use very little plant material so that the design has an uncluttered appearance.

Expressive Abstract

Plant material. In this style the plant material is used symbolically by the arranger to stand for something else and to express the arranger's ideas about a subject.

'Double the vision my eyes do see
And a double vision is always with me
To the inward eye, an old man grey
To the outward a thistle across the way.'
William Blake

It is fun to look at plant materials and consider what abstract idea they suggest. For example, a branch of a weeping willow may suggest 'sadness', a straight growing sansevieria leaf can stand for 'rigidity', a tiny pale pink rose may be 'delicacy' and a thorny branch could be 'cruelty'. As well as looking at the design qualities of plant material, the arranger should look at its symbolic qualities which can suggest abstract ideas. This is an interesting exercise.

Containers. These are often concealed as they

spaces made between the solids because they are equally important. Space can also be enclosed to give a pattern. The design should be very simple and often only one type of plant material may be used such as bulrushes, which can be bent and combined to form interesting spaces. A centre of interest, as in traditional arrangements, is not normal and round flowers may be used in any position for emphasis and to draw the eyes around the design.

Radiation, always used in traditional arrangements, should normally be avoided as it tends to

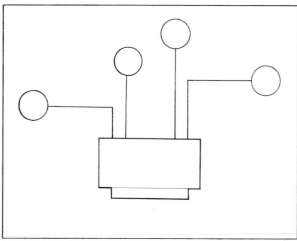

Lack of radiation in a design gives a more abstract appearance to the arrangement

can detract from the 'message'. If not concealed, they should be plain and simple, unless they play a part in the total expression of a subject. For example, in an interpretation of the subject 'Shelter' a container may be needed which is cave like in appearance.

Supports. Any support may be used which is suitable.

Design. The subject matter is not literally shown, for example, if creating an expressive abstract entitled 'Motherhood', the plant material should be symbolic of the arranger's own interpretation of motherhood. It might be an oval or egg-shaped piece of hollow wood with a small flower nestling at the bottom and this would symbolise protection. Alternatively, another arranger might see motherhood as domination and a large piece of plant material might envelop a smaller piece in a suffocating manner. The interpretation would *not* be abstract if a realistic figure of a Madonna was used with flowers around it. This would appear as a more literal and representational design. Simplicity is usually essential so that the message is clearly given.

'Birds in a Winter Tree'. This is a semi-abstract as it still has a slightly naturalistic appearance

Practical Arrangements

Practise interpreting the following subjects with plant material (and without figurines and other accessories to help): Storm, Youth, Dignity, Gaiety, Austerity.

It is also stimulating to create an arrangement and then give it an abstract name or ask members of the family or friends to do so.

PLAQUES AND SWAGS

The words 'flower arrangement' usually refer to plant material which is assembled in a container standing on a flat surface, such as a table. There are, however, other decorations of plant material made for hanging which can be included in the subject of flower arrangement. Perhaps they are not so much a style but a manner of construction and there are several methods.

A pressed flower picture is one type of hanging decoration and this has been described on page 57. Swags, plaques and garlands are other such decorations. These are fascinating to make and are very good for improving one's sense of design. They are especially effective for church festivals as they can be fixed high up on walls and pillars and be seen easily. Swags and plaques of dried plant material have been described with details of construction on pages 58 and 59.

Method of Making a Fresh Swag

1. Soak half a block of plastic foam in water and place this in a small polythene bag. Tie up the bag with string so that it exactly fits the block. Cut off any surplus polythene.
2. Cover this with a piece of wire netting so that the block is completely enclosed. Wire the cut sides of the netting together. Attach a long wire to the top of the netting and towards the back. This is for hanging the swag.
3. Push the stems into the plastic foam through the netting and polythene. If this seems difficult make

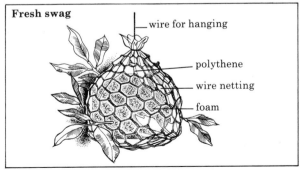

Fresh swag
wire for hanging
polythene
wire netting
foam

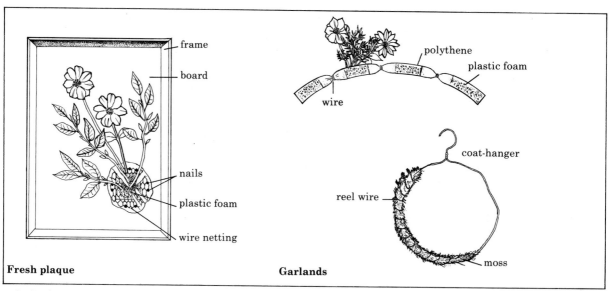

Fresh plaque

Garlands

a hole first with a meat skewer and then push in the softer stems.

It is helpful to cover the block first with flat, short-stemmed leaves (as for a table arrangement). Longer stems can be placed under these. It is important *not* to place any stem ends in the bottom of the plastic foam as the hole made in the polythene will allow water to leak out.

Method of Making a Fresh Plaque

A background will be needed for this. It can be framed or unframed. An old picture frame can be used with the backing covered with fabric. Alternatively, a new backing of polished wood can replace the old one. A piece of wood painted with matt paint is also effective. Any backing should be strong enough to hold several small nails. As the design is normally kept within the frame it is advisable to use a large one.
1. Cover half a block of plastic foam with polythene and netting as for the swag.
2. Attach this to the background by knocking 6 small nails into the backing so that the foam fits in between them and then wind a piece of reel wire around each nail and through the netting to hold the block firmly in place. Remember that once water is added to the foam it becomes much heavier. Moss may be used in place of foam and is lighter but does not hold as much water.
3. Push the stems of the plant material through the polythene and netting and into the foam or moss.

GARLANDS

Garlands are a very ancient form of decoration with plant material and the Egyptians, Romans and Greeks employed people who did nothing else but make them. Medieval paintings also show exquisite garlands of fruit and flowers and Grinling Gibbons' wood carvings of swags and garlands are famous. They can certainly be very beautiful but need patience for the construction. There are several methods.

A Flexible Garland

1. Cut a strip of heavy polythene the length required and 6 in. wide. Stitch the long sides together with a needle and thread or with a very long stitch on a sewing machine. Fill the polythene with wet moss or plastic foam. If the latter is used leave small gaps between pieces so that the garland bends easily. Twist a piece of wire tightly around the centre of each gap to prevent the plastic foam from slipping down.
2. Push the stems of plant material through the polythene. Use either woody stems or make a hole in the polythene first with a skewer. Hang up the garland with wires on nails or drape it around a statue, using wire to secure it in position.

A Stiffer Garland

1. Cut a long strip of wire netting, 1-in. mesh and 6 in. wide. The length depends on where the decoration is to be placed but it is sometimes easier to make several shorter lengths (each about 3 ft.) and join them together with wire.
2. Bend the netting over strips of plastic foam or florists' moss pulled out into a sausage. Leave spaces between the pieces of foam, if used, so that the garland will bend. Tie a length of reel wire tightly around the netting in between the pieces of foam. To conserve the water and prevent dripping, a piece of polythene may be placed on the netting (the same size as the netting) before

it is bent around the strips of moss or foam.
3. Push stems through the netting and into the moss or foam as before.

A Quick Garland

1. Pull florists' moss into a long strip.
2. Place a piece of heavy rope in the centre as a foundation.
3. Bind the moss around the rope with reel wire by holding the reel and simply winding it around the moss and rope.
4. Push the stems into the moss.

This is a quick way of making a garland of greenery but the mechanics are not as reliable as for the first two kinds. For a simple Christmas garland of long-lasting evergreens the foliage can be bound on to a rope without moss, but, of course, the result does not last as long.

A Circular Garland

The foundation can be made with a wire coat hanger bent into a circle or with a lampshade ring of about 18-in. diameter. Bind moss on to the hanger or ring with reel wire. Push the stems into the moss. Hang the garland by means of the coat-hanger hook (a bow of ribbon will conceal it) or a piece of reel wire attached to the lampshade ring.

A TOPIARY TREE

This type of construction is attractive for Christmas decorations and special events.

COMPONENTS
(A) 14-in. length of broomstick.
(B) 6-in.-diameter plastic pot without holes in the bottom.
(c) Plaster of Paris in powder form.
(D) Windscreen glass.
(E) Gold paint to paint the broomstick.
(F) Florists' moss, dampened.
(G) Wire netting, 1-in. mesh.
(H) 1 headless nail.
(I) $1\frac{1}{2}$ yd. of ribbon, $1\frac{1}{2}$ in. wide.

METHOD
1. Pour plaster of Paris powder into the pot until it is three quarters full and stir in cold water to obtain a consistency of thick cream.
2. Place the gilded broomstick in the centre. Hold it for a minute and make sure it is straight before the plaster sets (this takes a few minutes).

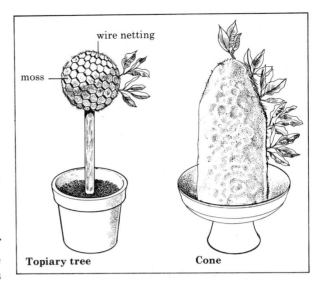

Topiary tree   Cone

3. Nail a long headless nail into the top of the broomstick (this may be done before placing it in the pot).
4. Wrap a ball of moss in the wire netting and impale this on the nail, pushing it well on.
5. Fill the ball with evergreens. Box is the most successful but yew or cupressus are also good. Very short pieces should be used.
6. Wrap the ball in polythene until it is required. It will keep fresh for several weeks.

This garland of artificial flowers, nuts and fruit makes a charming Christmas decoration especially when combined with the carved wooden statue

119

A topiary tree for Christmas. This is a long-lasting and fun-to-make decoration

if it is unattractive or it may be set inside another attractive pot.

CONE

This is another festive form of decoration which has been used for centuries, in fact, it started in Byzantium in about the 7th Century. It was previously made by binding flower stems on a stick and these gradually made the cone shape as more were added. This is still done in Mexico.

COMPONENTS
(A) Block of soaked plastic foam.
(B) Low container preferably with a stem, such as a stemmed cake plate.
(C) Foam pinholder secured with Plasticine in the container.

METHOD
1. Trim the foam into a rough triangle with a flat top and position it on the container.
2. Fill the plastic foam with flat leaves or box foliage.
3. Add flowers with short stems, flat flowers of the daisy type are the most successful.
4. Add fruits impaled on cocktail sticks. Grapes can be used if the stems are attached to long hairpins which can be inserted into the foam.

Dried Plant Material

Both the topiary tree and the cone can be made with dried, artificial or mixed plant material. When water is not needed for fresh plant material then plastic foam may be used which is not water retaining. This is sold in rounded and cone shapes.

INDIVIDUAL STYLE

We all have to copy at times in order to learn but as soon as possible you should try to bring your own personality into your work. Each artist is different from another because their lives, interests and experiences are different. We see things in various ways, which makes life more interesting, and conformity is dull and uninspiring. When trying to be individual, one makes mistakes but this is part of learning.

If you experiment and play with plant materials and have the courage to put them together in a different manner, the result may be new styles of your own.

7. Add flowers with strong stems such as single chrysanthemums. If desired, add fruit impaled on cocktail sticks or skewers. Small apples, tangerines, satsumas, small peppers and nuts are effective.
8. Tie a bow at the top of the stem and cover the plaster in the pot with windscreen glass or some other cover-up.

A plastic pot is necessary as the plaster will crack a china pot as it sets. The plastic pot may be gilded

Surroundings

Flowers are used for decoration in many places – in homes, churches, cathedrals, stately houses, schools, colleges, halls, hospitals, offices, restaurants and libraries. Wherever they are placed, they provide cheerful colouring, improve the appearance of stark walls and give a sense of care and attention. Flowers are rarely passed unnoticed and there are few who do not enjoy their beauty.

There are normally certain places in a building where flower arrangements can stand, such as on tables, shelves and windowsills. They can also be free standing on a raised plinth or pedestal and sometimes they may be hung on walls. It is important that the arrangement looks suitable for the position in which it is placed, as the setting and the design are seen together and it is impossible to separate them. When a flower arrangement is added to a room it immediately becomes part of the complete picture and inseparable from its surroundings and for this reason it should be co-ordinated with the existing architecture and furnishings. As these are more permanent and less changeable it is the flower arrangement which should be suited to the setting.

It is logical, before buying or cutting the flowers, to take a good look at the position where you plan to place flowers. This will indicate a desirable size and shape and suggest suitable colouring.

Position

If there is a choice of placement for a flower arrangement, the following points should be considered:

1. Flowers do not last well when placed over a hot fire or radiator, directly in sunshine or strong light. Cooler and shadier positions are better.
2. Flowers cannot be clearly seen when placed in front of a window with the light behind them, except at night. A plain wall or alcove usually provides the best background.
3. Flowers may be used to draw attention away from an ugly feature or ungainly furnishings in a room. They can also decorate a vacant wall or corner giving a well-furnished appearance.
4. If one arrangement seems insufficient for a

room thought should be given to the number necessary. One or two larger designs often look better than many smaller ones which tend to make a room look fussy and too dressed up.
5. Where beautiful furnishings are already present in a room, it is better not to hide these and instead to look for available spaces in between them. It is also possible to complement these beautiful things by the colour and shape of the flower arrangements.
6. Furniture is usually placed in a room for a functional purpose. It may need to hold a lamp, books, ashtrays, cups and saucers, glasses, magazines. For this reason the flower arrangement should not take up the entire space available and room should be left for these other things.

Size

Once the position for a flower arrangement has been decided the next step is to consider the amount of space available within the limits imposed by existing furnishings. For example, a table with a painting centred above it may need either a low arrangement under the painting or an arrangement on each side of it. It is helpful to think of the space available as a three-dimensional block to be pleasingly filled with flowers. It is easy to overcrowd or underfill it, which makes the setting seem very small or far too big. A large bare wall has no boundaries and the arrangement will probably need lifting on a pedestal to make it appear big enough for the wall.

Once a size has been decided for the arrangement, then a container and plant material can be chosen in scale. Larger designs need bigger containers, flowers and leaves and smaller designs need smaller containers and plant material.

Shape

The available space for a flower arrangement will also suggest its shape. A narrow alcove will need a slim vertical design. A low coffee table will need one suitable to talk over and the flower arrangement should look attractive from above. Long refectory tables may look best with a slender garland. Usually the shape of the space available can be approximately repeated in the shape of the arrangement.

Colour

The colour scheme of a room is a major consideration in deciding on the colour for the flower arrangement. In a room which has been decorated in many colours or patterns a monochromatic (one-coloured) design may be the most striking. A dull room may need more variety in the flower colours. Sometimes it is helpful to the overall appearance of the room to repeat the colour of a furnishing accessory. In a room decorated in tints, hues and shades of one colour – say blue – an arrangement of flowers in orange, the complement of blue, is quite dramatic.

A lot depends on the climate. In very hot weather a cool arrangement of blues and greens is restful. In a cold climate the reds and oranges are full of warmth and are more cheerful than the cool colours.

In a room which contains many flower arrangements a link between them in colour gives a better effect of harmony, for example, a hall with several pedestal arrangements may look better if one design is red, one pink and one orange. These colours have a close relationship and a sense of co-ordination is given.

Style

This is an important consideration when a room is already furnished in a distinctive style. For example, a period arrangement in an antique container does not suit a very modern room and similarly an abstract design is unlikely to suit a Victorian drawing room.

Often one hears someone say that they dislike a certain style of flower arrangement, but what they usually mean is that they dislike that style in their own home surroundings. Most people will agree with a style when it appears suitable for its setting. Harmony is achieved in a flower arrangement when all the components agree. Similarly, as the arrangement and the setting are inseparable they, too, should agree in size, shape, colour and style.

Lighting

Good lighting improves the appearance of any flower arrangement. Spotlights are particularly effective directed on to a design, but care should be taken that the light is not close to the plant material or it will wilt. A softly lit alcove is a beautiful setting and draws attention to the flowers. Fluorescent lighting can be disastrous and take all the sparkle from the colours. Tungsten electric lighting is kinder unless a warm white or pink fluorescent light is used.

Rooms with poor lighting need colours which are luminous and show up well in the darkness, such as the tints, white, yellow and orange. Violets, blues and greens are often lost in dim lighting.

Many traditional homes have built-in alcoves or shelves for flowers. Modern homes could also have such facilities so that there is a definite place for a flower arrangement, with a suitable background and lighting. This has been a feature of Chinese and Japanese homes for centuries. Plants and flowers are highly decorative and this would help considerably to soften the outlines of modern rooms, which can appear very stark.

Special Settings

STATELY HOMES

Exhibitions of flower arrangements are often held in stately homes and you may be asked to help with the decoration. It is probable that there will be a designer who will indicate where the arrangements are to go and the colours and shape to be used. If not and you are 'on your own', remember that the room will probably contain many decorative features and precious objects. It is important to complement and not hide these. There are often many colours and it may be effective to use only one of these in the design of flowers.

The rooms are normally furnished with traditional furniture and the designs should also be in this style. If a definite period is reflected in the furnishings then an arrangement in the manner of this period will give a wonderful atmosphere.

Permission should always be obtained to place arrangements on antique furniture and to move anything of value. Very special care should also be taken to avoid water damage on polished surfaces, such as table tops and floors, and sheets of polythene must be used to protect them while working on the arrangement.

CHURCHES AND CATHEDRALS

People are often asked to arrange flowers in a church and it is a help to know something about this.

The Position for Arrangements

More people will see the flowers if they are lifted up and not at table level. Many churches have pedestals and plinths available. Often there are shelves which may be used and an arrangement can look beautiful if the plant material cascades down from the shelf. Wall arrangements in the form of swags are effective but nails should not be knocked into the wall without permission. Often there are existing nails or knobs for hanging. The top of the font is a good place for a flower arrangement but some clergy do not like the font used for this purpose. It is also important that the arrangements are positioned so that they enhance rather than hide any beautiful features or furnishings. They can complement these in colour and shape.

The Clergy and Congregation

When considering the placement of flowers the advice and wishes of the clergy should always be sought and particular attention given to ensuring that arrangements do not impede the clergy or congregation.

Stability and neatness are essential in the design so that arrangements are not easily knocked over and do not fall over because of poor mechanics. This is distressing for everyone and not conducive to the atmosphere of worship. It is sometimes necessary to wire an arrangement, using a long piece of reel wire, to the existing (and stable) furnishings.

Style

The style of the arrangement should suit the style of the church whether it is traditional or modern. A clear-cut outline is usually the most effective because of the distance from which the arrangements are generally seen. Details are not obvious and the normally dim lighting also blurs shapes. For this reason massed arrangements may be the most suitable.

Size

Cathedrals are so huge that flower arrangements appear dwarfed. No flowers seem big enough for the setting. It is usually best to concentrate on the immediate surroundings for the design as often the cathedral cannot be seen as a complete picture anyway. A group of several arrangements can be effective and these should be co-ordinated, for example, with different heights and sizes to give variety. In a church the normal considerations apply – the size should suit the setting, the distance of viewing and the movements of people.

Colours

The lighting is usually rather dim and colours that show up well in poor lighting should be used. Colours with a lot of weight do not 'lift' and with the high roofs and heavy fabric and furnishings of a church the lighter colours with less weight seem more pleasing. A clear contrast in value between the flowers and the background is a help as the design is more easily seen. This means that against a white wall darker flowers will be better and against a dark wall lighter flowers will show up well.

It is essential when arranging church flowers to keep going a long way back from them and to look at the design from a position in a pew is helpful. The shape and colours can look so

Two pedestals for a January wedding of foliage of Western hemlock, *Elaeagnus pungens aurea* and bergenia with chrysanthemums, carnations and lilies

different from a distance and you may have many a surprise. Altar cloths are used in different colours at various times and these should be considered when the flower colours are chosen.

Containers and Mechanics

The containers, other than the altar vases, need to be bigger than those used in the average home. Most churches have a collection. Stone and china urns, garden vases of stone and fibreglass, lined wooden tubs, pedestals, large baskets (especially for a country church), troughs, china soup tureens, vegetable bowls and Victorian wash bowls are all suitable. Modern stoneware containers are effective in newer churches. Old standard lamp pedestals can soon be converted by having a small shelf fixed to the top on which a container can be placed, and this lifts a flower arrangement so that it can be seen.

As the flowers are often seen from different angles the mechanics should be very well hidden. It is not wise to use your own pinholders because they may get lost, wire netting and plastic foam are disposable and can be forgotten. Altar vases can be difficult with regard to mechanics. If wire netting is used, lift it well above the top of the container so that there is plenty of support for the stems.

Plant Material

Long lasting plant material is important since the flowers are often only changed once a week. It is usually necessary for the cost to be low. For this reason foliage is extremely useful, especially yellow-green leaves which show up well in the dim lighting. A collection of preserved foliage will also stretch the flowers in the winter. Plants are rarely used because they need good lighting to grow well, but where there is a suitable window, pot-et-fleur makes an excellent form of decoration. Fruit arrangements could also be used more often.

Altar Flowers

Flowers on the altar need special consideration. Often the setting is already highly decorative and with the Cross, and perhaps candlesticks, there can be little spare room. For these reasons very simple arrangements with flowers of a bold shape are usually better. It is normal to enhance the Cross and not to make the flower arrangements dominant. Sometimes a pair of crescents or Hogarth curves can direct attention to the Cross. Care should be taken when arranging the flowers

A swag of fresh plant material wired to the altar rail for a wedding decoration

to keep the altar cloths quite clean and a polythene sheet should be used to cover them while arranging.

Weddings

On this occasion it is the bride's day and the choice of colour for flowers should be hers. However, it is helpful to visit the church with her to give some advice based on the availability of flowers, the colours of the bridal party's dresses and the colours of the church walls and carpeting.

An effective colour scheme can be white flowers with a touch of colour similar to the bridesmaids' dresses or the bouquets.

Harvest Festivals

This is an occasion when many people enjoy helping to decorate the church. Consequently there are often too many small arrangements. If you are in charge, try grouping several designs together, or have a number of people working on one large design. Swags and garlands look lovely on pillars and walls. Cones of fruit can be made for pedestals in place of the usual flowers.

Christmas

Glittered and artificial plastic plant materials do not usually suit a church setting and evergreens, berries and flowers seem more harmonious. Candles may be incorporated but if they are to be lit they should be kept well away from the plant material. Cones of evergreens, studded with flowers and fruit, garlands and swags give a change of style which is enjoyable. Small oil lamps are reasonably safe and can be incorporated into arrangements of evergreens and flowers.

TABLE ARRANGEMENTS

This term refers to arrangements used to decorate tables for seated meals. They are probably the most popular type of arrangement used in a home as most hostesses like to place a few fresh flowers on the table, and therefore they need extra consideration. There are also special events, such as the annual Christmas dinner of some organisation, when decorations are attractive on the tables. There are several points to be considered when making these arrangements:

Simplicity. Cooking the meal is the most important job for a hostess and the flower arrangement must usually be done quickly in the midst of getting the meal ready. A simple arrangement is therefore the most practical and sensible. The following list of quick ideas may be helpful.

(A) Fruit placed on a low container with a few glycerined leaves.

(B) Two or three beautiful flowers and a few leaves in a shell. Plastic foam can be used for speed.

(C) A few flowers floating on water in a low dish. This is lovely for a hot day.

(D) One or two orchid tubes of water containing the stems of flowers, which can be placed amongst a grouping of fruit or of shells and coral.

(E) A low bowl of small house plants. A few flowers can be added.

(F) Place a small block of plastic foam on a foam pinholder secured to a stemmed cake plate. Stand a chunky candle on the top of the foam and cut short-stemmed flowers from two stems of spray chrysanthemums, inserting them below the candle.

Size. The table is in use for eating purposes and not for showing off flowers and for this reason room must be left for the food and its serving. Any arrangement of flowers should be small and neat and not so large and overflowing that branches dangle in the soup. The arrangement is to make the table more inviting and perhaps to fill a gap in the centre of the table. It is something for the guests to look at and may even be a conversation piece but it should not be so dominant that it becomes overwhelming. A reasonable guide is for the flower arrangement to take up no more than one fifth of the table top, depending on the type of meal and the number of people to be seated.

Grooming. Probably no other flower arrange-

A centrepiece for a table decoration of two orchids and a few beautiful shells

ment in a home setting is looked at for as long, or at such close quarters, as a table arrangement at a seated meal. For this reason and also because of the close proximity of food, grooming is essential. It is not appetising to watch greenfly climbing over foliage or earwigs dropping from flowers and so insect-infested plant material should not be used. All foliage should be swished through soapy water and damaged leaves should be trimmed off.

Shape. There are few things more irritating than trying to talk around, through or over a large flower arrangement in the centre of a table. Conversation is an important part of a meal in company and the flowers should never interfere with this. A low arrangement is the most suitable, which means that the design should look attractive from above. Normally people sit all round the table and this means that the design should also be pleasing from every side. It is helpful to walk around the table looking at the arrangement when you have finished it and also to sit down briefly to have the same angle of viewing as the guests.

The shape of the table will suggest a shape for the flower arrangement. A round or oval table may look best with a design of similar shape. A rectangular table may need a design which is longer than it is wide. A long narrow table may need a garland down the centre or arrangements at both ends.

Placement. Many people like a central placement for the flowers but, as a change, other positions may be tried.

Colours. The colours of the flowers should suit the colours in the china as well as the room in general. The decoration on a plate may also give

A simple and quickly made table arrangement consisting of a chunky candle with single chrysanthemums

The Table

The area taken up by the table top is relatively large compared with the arrangement and therefore the colour of the cloth should be chosen with care. White cloths have been used more often than not in the past but coloured ones can contribute to beautiful colour schemes when combined with flowers and china. Brilliant colours are tiring on the eye but soft, subtle ones are very pleasing and dark shades of green, violet, navy, brown and red show off flowers surprisingly well. It is not difficult to make or buy coloured cloths or to dye old white ones. For special occasions second 'see-through' cloths, made of lace or other delicate fabrics, are very glamorous. Mats can give many colour changes and the wood of the table is an attractive background for flowers when a tablecloth is not used.

a key to the type of plant material. Plain china gives more possibilities than patterned for varying the flower arrangements.

Colour Scheme Suggestions

(A) On a hot day, white flowers and china on a navy blue cloth with lime-green candles and foliage.
(B) For Christmas, a deep red cloth and an arrangement of variegated holly, red berries, small white chrysanthemums or red roses, with gilded foliage and white and gold china.
(C) A violet cloth with pink and mauve flowers, grey foliage.
(D) A brown cloth with orange and pink flowers, brown candles and modern china.
(E) A grey cloth with deeper pink flowers and grey or lime-green foliage, silver and white china.

Lighting

Candlelight is often used for evening meals and as it is a weak form of lighting the colours of the flowers should be carefully considered. Those which do not show up well in dim lighting, such as blue, violet and dark green, will disappear almost totally in candlelight. The tints of colours will show up better, also clear yellows, oranges, flames and, of course, white. Candles may be bought in beautiful colours but they can easily dominate the flowers. Those which blend well are leaf-coloured greens, cream and the more subtle colours.

Special Occasions

There are times when people are especially honoured such as on birthdays and wedding anniversaries. It is then appropriate to use colours, styles and plant material to suit the event

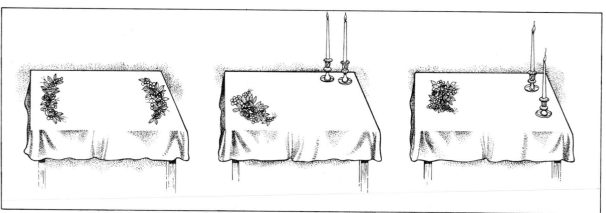

There are various positions in which arrangements of flowers can be placed on a table

and the people concerned. For example, a table decoration for a golden wedding anniversary could use gold roses in a traditional style; a teenager's birthday party could have a modern decoration using several brilliant colours with a small gift incorporated as an accessory.

Buffet Table Designs

At a buffet party the guests are normally standing and the flower arrangements should be higher than those used for a seated meal so that they can be seen at eye level. Plenty of room is usually needed for the food and designs which take up a lot of table space can be in the way. Suitable containers to lift the flower arrangements are candlesticks, candelabra and pedestal-type containers.

Arrangements for Functions

When an organisation to which you belong holds a large dinner you may be asked to help with the flower arrangements used for decorating the dining tables. There is not always much money allowed for this purpose and so simple ideas are necessary, especially in winter months when flowers are more expensive. If many similar designs are to be made it is sensible for one good arranger to make up an arrangement for the rest of the team to copy.

A larger arrangement may be made for the 'top' table and then smaller ones which are economical can be made as follows:
(A) Variegated foliage with two or three small flowers added. Containers can be plastic lids from jars (saved beforehand) with plastic foam and a cap of wire netting for the mechanics.
(B) Two lemons and an orange or apple, held together with cocktail sticks and placed on well washed and polished leaves of long lasting ivy or laurel, without a container. The fruit may be used afterwards.
(C) When a raffle is held for the flowers and there is a little more money available, small containers such as baskets can be used. Place half a round of soaked plastic foam into a little polythene bag and tie up the open end. Cover this with small mesh wire netting which is held to the basket with reel wire. Garden flowers look pretty in a basket.
(D) Candlesticks may be easily available especially if the event is held in a restaurant. Cut a small hole in the centre of half a round of plastic foam. Push a candle through this, slender end first. The candle gets thicker nearer its base and the foam will not slip down. Add flowers with very

An arrangement for a Christmas buffet table using a pineapple, tangerines, apples, holly and blue cedar

short stems to make a ring of flowers. Place the candle in a candlestick.

HOSPITALS

We send flowers to people in hospital because they say for us so much that we feel but cannot easily put into words. Flowers are important to the patients because they realise that they are not forgotten and also because they are something to look at, especially when someone is too ill to do

127

An arrangement on a candle

plastic foam

anything else. The flowers become a link with nature and the outside world from which patients are cut off temporarily. They also add needed colour and cheer up the hospital wards.

It is probable that flowers mean more to people when they are in hospital than at any other time and it is therefore well worth spending time and care on their selection. Flower shops will send flower arrangements in place of the usual cut flowers, but if you have time to arrange and deliver them yourself then it shows your own care and interest. Nurses are usually delighted to receive

Locker-top arrangements to send to hospital for winter (left), spring (centre top), Christmas (centre bottom) and all the year round (right)

flowers ready arranged as it saves so much of their valuable time.

There are certain things to be thought about when arranging flowers for hospital.

Transportation. This must be simple and easy. Extras such as bases and accessories are only a nuisance and should not be included in the design.

The mechanics. These must be very firm because the arrangement is often moved about. It can also distress a patient to see it fall over and cause extra work. Wire netting and plastic foam are the most suitable mechanics as they are disposable. Valuable pinholders might be mislaid.

Containers. Containers should be disposable or should be given as gifts to the patients because it is extra work for someone to have to keep track of them and return them to the owners. There are many inexpensive containers which are excellent and easily available, including small baskets, plastic urns and goblets, inexpensive modern pottery. Alternatively, the flowers can be arranged in plastic foam in a plastic saucer. This costs little and the container can be hidden by the plant material.

A neat style. This is the most successful as trails of plant material do get in the way, especially on locker tops. Small arrangements made for a locker top or bedside table are attractive and most acceptable as they are more personal than cut flowers which are placed further away in the ward.

Plant material. This should be well conditioned and long lasting as hospital wards are normally warmer than the average home and flowers can soon fade.

Suggestions are:

(A) A small arrangement of dried plant materials or a tiny plaque or swag which can be taken home by the patient later.

(B) A plant which is acceptable for the same reason. Cut flowers may be added to it to make a small pot-et-fleur. The plant will remain and still be attractive when the flowers have faded and been removed.

(C) A fresh foliage arrangement which will last longer than flowers, or a design using a lot of foliage with a few flowers which can easily be replaced.

(D) A glycerined foliage arrangement to make a semi-permanent design with the addition of a few fresh flowers.

(E) A small twist of driftwood which will be enjoyed by some patients. A few flowers and some foliage may be added.

Colours. These should not be overpowering for a patient who is very ill. Yellow, red and orange

A neat arrangement for an oval table of roses, freesias and Japanese honeysuckle foliage

can be very brilliant and advancing. Calmer blues and greens are more restful. The cheerful advancing colours may be more suitable and stimulating for the recuperative stage.

Water. To save the work of changing the water in a container a mild disinfectant can be added ($\frac{1}{4}$ teaspoonful of chlorhexidine to 1 pint of water). This discourages the growth of bacteria and can be a great help to the busy hospital staff. It is sensible to add a note that this has been done and also any other instructions with regard to watering the flowers or plants such as 'This water contains disinfectant and need not be changed'. 'Please add water to this arrangement on arrival.' 'Pour a little water on the top of the plastic foam every day.'

The Therapeutic Value of Flowers

This is something which is under-valued. Patients who have a long stay in hospital may be well enough to do something with their hands and could do flower arrangements. A 'kit' may be a useful present, in place of cut flowers or flowers ready arranged. The kit could consist of one of the following groups of components. A short clear list of instructions for a beginner may also be included.

FOR A FRESH FLOWER ARRANGEMENT
A small round of soaked plastic foam.
A plastic saucer.
Flower scissors.
A few fresh flowers.
Some foliage.

FOR A DRIED FLOWER ARRANGEMENT
A small round of dry plastic foam.
A plastic saucer or small container.
A few pieces of dried plant material.
Flower scissors.

FOR A PLAQUE
A fabric covered plaque (these can be bought).
Dried plant material.
Flower scissors.
Glue.

FOR A PRESSED FLOWER PICTURE
A small picture frame with the backboard ready covered with paper or fabric.
Copydex or a latex type adhesive.
Pressed plant material in an envelope.
Small scissors.

Any of these gifts may well start a patient, man or woman, on a new interest in life and this can be of great therapeutic value.

Arranging Flowers in Hospital

Many flower arrangers volunteer their services and go into hospitals every week to arrange the cut flowers that have been sent. This is a great help to the staff. It also gives the flower arranger practice with flowers she might not have otherwise.

Large pedestals are often effective in the wards and concentrate the flowers in one position, out of the way of the movements of the medical staff, which should never be impeded by the flowers. It is also a good way to combine the many cut flowers which arrive, although the patients should be asked if they mind their flowers being grouped with others. Some people prefer to have their own flowers placed near to them. The sister in charge of the ward will show you where to work and suggest the placement of the flowers. Her wishes should be respected.

It is helpful to get a collection together of suitable containers and mechanics which are kept at the hospital. Friends may donate containers, or a coffee morning can provide the proceeds to buy some. It is helpful to take in some of your own foliage as this is rarely sent with cut flowers and can improve the appearance of the flower arrangement considerably.

LIBRARIES

Most functional rooms can be improved by the addition of flowers and plants. They soften the architectural lines of the room, which can be stark, and give a feeling of care and attention. It is important, however, that flower arrangements do not interfere with the movement of people or the business in hand. A librarian may be pleased to have a flower arrangement placed in the library regularly by flower club members. This, with his permission, could have a notice of the next club meeting placed beside it and may bring in new members.

SCHOOLS

Children love flowers and will often take some to school. This is a time when a love of nature can so easily be stimulated and fostered. Many flower arrangers talk of their childhood days as being an inspiration for flower arrangement in their adult life and tell of walks as a child through country lanes and looking at flowers on the way.

A child seems to have more time to stop and

look and awareness and perception of beauty can be encouraged. Therefore, it seems a pity to place the flowers, that children lovingly bring to school, haphazardly in the nearest jam jar. Arranging them pleasingly can be something taught from the beginning and the design can be quite simple. There are times during the school hours when children need things to do and this could be a delightful occupation, and save the time of the busy teacher. She may be able to give one or two lessons in simple flower arrangement but, alternatively, a suitable person (perhaps one of the mothers) may be able to come into school and give a few lessons. Many schools would welcome this at a time when the staff are busy with such things as examination paper marking. Older girls enjoy practice meetings with a flower arranger and can bring their own materials if a clear list is given beforehand. Some of them will go on to take the flower arranging badge of the Girl Guides and others may do flower arrangement as a subject under the Duke of Edinburgh Awards scheme.

Flower arrangement need not be a fringe subject in school as it can teach so much about combining colours, shapes and textures, it can develop the 'seeing eye' and give a knowledge of nature. It can also teach children to value and conserve natural things of beauty and this may be a great help to the future preservation of the environment.

It is wise for a flower arranger who would like to work with children, to speak to the head teacher of the school.

A long-lasting foliage arrangement for a library of ivy, cupressus, *Fatsia japonica*, aspidistra and house-leek

Mechanics and Containers

These can be difficult as the school or children may have none and lack the money to buy them. Interesting containers can be made in the handwork lesson or the pottery class with the co-operation of the teacher. There are many simple containers to be made which cost little. The school may invest in some pinholders for older children – the younger ones can hurt themselves on the sharp pins. Wire netting and moss can be used otherwise. A box of plastic foam can be bought by the school at a cheaper price through a wholesaler.

What to Teach Children

The younger children, from about seven years of age, can learn:
1. To condition plant material (leaving out burning stem ends).

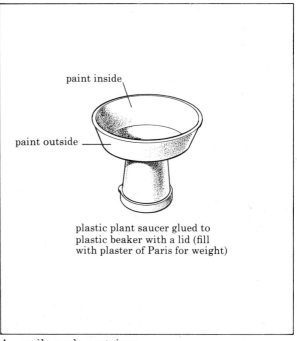

An easily made container

Above: Autumn plant material in an old oil-lamp base. The arrangement, lamp and painting are composed together to make a harmonious design
Opposite: Harmony in colour and style between the flower arrangement and its setting

2. Grooming and trimming with flower scissors.
3. How to support the stems.
4. To make simple arrangements with the emphasis on good spacing, cutting stems different lengths and turning flowers.
5. To be aware of the colours and textures of plant material.

Children younger than seven may not be able to handle scissors but they can still learn to space flowers, turn the heads in various directions and to include leaves. Older children from eight years of age can learn all the things an adult learns and will normally pick up instructions very quickly. Those of eleven and upwards will enjoy pressing flowers for pictures, drying and preserving, making plaques and swags. Christmas decorations are popular with all children as they have something to take home to their parents and glittering and spraying is great fun for them. (This should normally be avoided with the kindergarten children or chaos may result.)

Style is usually not important in a school setting and the older children can learn all the styles. They may take special interest in period arrangements which are a link with history lessons. The students in the top class can be taught to link flower arrangements with their surroundings so that they can create designs suitable for the school hall for assembly and for special occasions. Landscape arrangements are especially easy and economical for young people to make and they love them. At any age children's interest can be stimulated by looking at a collection of things which can be included in a flower arrangement such as pebbles, driftwood, lichen and stones. A labelled grouping of objects from one habitat could give them ideas for a landscape design, using easily available plant material.

A scrapbook of pictures of flower arrangements can be started at any age. Growing plants and germinating seeds may already be an activity in the class, but if not this can be introduced in relation to flower arrangement. It is important for children to learn that plant material can be grown easily to use in flower arrangements. They may also be encouraged to look for such things as driftwood and shells on outings and holidays. This makes the holiday more enjoyable, provides an activity and increases their perception and awareness of all the lovely things in the world around us. Very soon all the flower arrangements in a school will become more attractive as a result of the greater interest.

OFFICES

The functional nature of an office can give an especially sterile atmosphere which is greatly relieved by the addition of plants and flowers. Although the flower arrangements should not interfere with business, they can be a cheering influence on the staff and make the office seem more cared for. Neat simple arrangements are the most suitable as they are not easily knocked over. A small bowl of bright flowers arranged on the boss' table may well put him in a good mood and is certainly a welcome for visitors. It should be placed away from papers, of course, and be very stable. Flowers in a waiting room are especially cheerful.

HALLS

Large spectacular arrangements lifted on pedestals are the most effective for large halls as low ones will not be seen. The sides of the stage are often good positions and flowers may be combined with growing plants. Grouped designs or one very big one give a large splash of colour which is usually more effective than many small arrangements individually placed.

Advancing colours are the most suitable for large rooms and bold outlines are necessary as details are not seen. Wall arrangements hung high up are easily seen providing they can be attached successfully to the wall, without causing damage.

Spotlighting, if available, is excellent for drawing attention to the flower arrangements and can be very dramatic. Different coloured bulbs or acetate film can be used. 'Catherine wheel' lights, which change colour, are sometimes part of the props available in halls and the changing colours are exciting when seen moving over white plant material.

Show Work

Once you have learnt the basic skills of flower arrangement and know something about design, then it is stimulating to enter one of the local flower arrangement shows. These are usually staged by a flower arrangement club or by a horticultural society which includes classes for flower arrangement in addition to horticulture.

Exhibiting at a show can get you out of a rut and widen your experience. Many people tend to use the same container and similar colours and styles in set positions in their homes. This can get boring and a show which asks for something new to test one's skills and knowledge can give fresh interest. It is fun to work with other flower arrangers at staging time and many new friends are made in this way. There is also much to be learnt from other flower arrangers, the work they do and the way they do it. Foliage is often exchanged, bases and mechanics lent and opinions sought.

It is always important to enter a show for the experience and enjoyment and not with the sole idea of winning a prize, which is a bonus. There is then no disappointment and afterwards you will find that you have stretched your ability and learnt a lot. The judge is usually a person with wide experience and sound knowledge who should be trusted although you may not agree with the results. The judge will spend a long time looking at all the exhibits and seeing things that are not apparent to anyone else during a brief look. Sometimes comments will be put on your entry card and these are most helpful. Often the judge stays behind to talk to exhibitors and this is the time to ask for an opinion of your work.

Procedure for Entering a Show

At first, everything may seem strange but confidence comes when you know the procedure. Before entering your first show, visit one that is being held locally to look at the general organisation. You may also be able to find a friend who is used to entering shows and who is willing to use you as a 'dog's-body' when staging. When you have decided to 'have a go' yourself, then send for the schedule of the show, which should give you all the information you need. If it does not, telephone the show secretary whose name and address should be printed on the schedule and who will also help you if there is anything you do not understand (but remember show secretaries are busy people). When you have decided which classes to enter, fill in very carefully the entry form that comes with the schedule, and send it, with the money stated, to the show secretary, by the date shown on the form.

Choosing Classes to Enter

Each schedule usually contains a number of competitive classes. You will be eligible to enter some of them, but others may be limited to entries from clubs or advanced arrangers. Often there is a class for people who have never won a prize in a show before and this may be a good one with which to start.

Decide which classes inspire you and for which you have suitable containers and accessories. It is wise to enter two classes in your first show as more than this can be confusing until you have had some practice. If you only enter one class you may find you are too preoccupied with it and a second entry can take your mind off the first one so that it can be looked at again with a fresh eye.

Planning the Exhibit

Some time before the show you will need to think about your entries. It is wise not to copy other flower arrangers' work, or a picture in a book, as you will be marked down for lack of originality. Expensive flowers are not necessary and, in fact, you will be surprised how many prizes are won by entries with only two or three flowers, and sometimes none at all. The cost of the flowers is not considered by the judge who may give more prizes to restrained arrangements using simple plant material.

When you have a quiet moment, write down all the things you associate with the titles of the classes you will be entering. It is helpful to use headings.

Right: A traditional triangular arrangement of *Acer platanoides*, yellow tulips and chrysanthemums of the variety Bonnie Jean in a figurine container
Left: An arrangement in the modern style for a party occasion. The plant material is elaeagnus foliage, chrysanthemums, fruit, roses, geraniums and strelitzia with peacock's feathers

The class could be called *The Lakeside.*

COLOURS	Quiet greens, blues, browns
PLANT MATERIAL	Reeds, iris and other water plants
CONTAINER	Large low bowl which can feature water
BASE	None
MECHANICS	Large pinholder
ACCESSORY/IES	Stones
STYLE	Naturalistic
DRAPE OR BACKGROUND	None
RESEARCH	Find out the plants which grow by a lakeside.

The headings on the left may be used for all class titles. The words written on the right will vary with each title and with each arranger and there will be quite different words, for example, for a class called 'Interpreting Covent Garden' and one called 'Tranquillity'.

Sometimes it is necessary to look up a word to make quite sure of the meaning or to find out some information from books in the library and this is covered by the heading 'research'. For example, a class might have the title 'A Victorian Design' and then it could be necessary to look through some books on Victoriana to see the style of arrangement and types of plant material used. This homework leads flower arrangers along many interesting paths and they learn all kinds of things apart from flower arrangement, which is one more bonus gained from entering shows.

The list will prove most helpful as it prepares your mind so that you can decide what arrangement to do. It also provides a check list when you are packing everything to take to the show.

Following the Schedule

The class title gives you a clue as to the type of arrangement that is expected. There may also be other words following the title. These *must* be regarded if you are not to be eliminated from the competition. For example, if you enter a class which asks for foliage *only* and you add flowers then the judge cannot consider your entry for a prize and will write on your entry card 'Not according to schedule'. This is very disappointing when you have spent thought, time and money on your arrangement. Be careful then to look at every word. At home you may do anything you like when arranging plant material, but in a competitive show it is necessary to follow the

schedule if your entry is to be considered eligible for a prize. This discipline, however, is very good as it usually improves your flower arranging.

It is important to read every word in the title and all the words which follow. For example, 'Autumn Splendour' is not quite the same as 'Autumn Elegance' and different designs will be expected. Both titles contain the word autumn and so plant material that is normally seen in the autumn will be necessary but splendour and elegance have different meanings. Splendour suggests rich colouring and rather grand, massed flowers, whereas elegance suggests a more streamlined and sophisticated effect. It is wise to look up the words of the title in the dictionary to confirm their meaning.

Some organisations, and in particular The National Association of Flower Arrangement Societies of Great Britain, and the National Council of State Garden Clubs of the U.S.A., have booklets containing definitions of words which are often used in show schedules. These can be very helpful because they define what can be included in an exhibit. If, for example, 'fruit' is to be used in the class then the booklet will say if such things as berries and pine cones are allowed. If the show you enter is to be judged according to any special definitions this will be stated on the show schedule. It is sensible to obtain a copy of this booklet and read it beforehand. The show secretary will be able to tell you where to buy it.

It is usually wise to enter classes which do not include many words after the title as each word can be a pitfall. For example 'A basket arrangement of foliage and fruit' sounds simple but it may mean that you must look up the words basket, foliage, fruit, and even arrangement to be sure of their definition, and also that you must not include flowers in the design. A class titled 'Autumn Bounty' without any other words following, gives more scope and less chance of going wrong.

The size of the space allowed for your exhibit is normally given and it is important to keep within this area or again you may be disqualified. It is necessary for the show committee to allocate space so that they can stage the show pleasingly and allow everyone a similar amount of space. Colours of backgrounds are usually given in the show schedule and these should be considered when planning your entry. Some classes state that no accessories are allowed. It is important to read what this term includes so that you do not use an accessory unwittingly.

It is essential then:
1. To read the show schedule carefully.

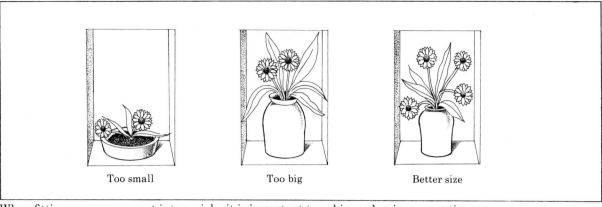

| Too small | Too big | Better size |

When fitting an arrangement into a niche it is important to achieve pleasing proportions

2. To make sure that you understand what is meant by each word, with the help of the *Handbook of Schedule Definitions* used by the show and stated in the schedule.

3. To ask, if you are in doubt about anything. The show secretary should be able to help before the show and the judge can be asked after the show.

Preparation

A mock-up. After you have planned your exhibit, it is wise to have a 'mock-up', which means setting your arrangement out and trying the components in various positions. It is helpful to draw a rectangle with chalk on the garage wall (or some other place where it will not matter) which is the same size as the space allowed by the schedule for your exhibit. Then you can try the intended arrangement against this chalk outline. It is necessary to fill the space allowed with an exhibit which is in pleasing proportion. At some shows a niche of cardboard or wood is provided, at others only a background. Whether or not there is a framework, the exhibit should not be too large or too small for the space allowed. If it is, then it may lose marks. It is advisable not to extend over the edge of the table, or to touch the walls of the niche, or the marking tapes separating the exhibits, with plant material. The whole volume of space should be filled adequately, bearing in mind that some designs use more space *within* them than others. The following suggestions may be used as guides for size but they should be adapted to the materials used.

1. If the container is to be visible it should be about one-third of the height or width of the back panel, whichever is the largest measurement. This gives space above the container for a pleasing length of plant material. If a base is used it should be included in the measurement of the container.

2. The margin between the inside walls of the niche (or the space allowed) and the exhibit should be about one-twelfth of the height or width of the space. For example, if a space is allowed of height 36 in. and width 24 in., then a pleasing margin to leave around the exhibit is 3 in. on either side and 2 in. at the top.

It is unnecessary to use exactly the same plant materials for a mock-up as you will use in the show, but substitutes can give an idea of shape, colour and size. Leave the design in place for a few days and pop back now and again to look at it. This is very helpful as you usually look at it with fresh eyes each time and can correct faults.

Collecting materials. Sometimes it is necessary to borrow containers and accessories, and other flower arrangers are normally very willing to share some of their possessions. It is not always possible to have exactly the right thing yourself.

Flowers should be ordered well in advance from the florist or nursery. You should give alternatives as it is not always possible to get exactly the flower or colour that you would like.

Cleaning. A few days before the show clean the containers, bases and accessories, as good grooming is essential to a pleasing exhibit.

Collect your plant material one or two days before the show and make sure it is well conditioned. Floppy, wilted plant material will not be considered for a prize and it also spoils the appearance of the show for the general public. All foliage should be well washed and groomed. Damaged leaves and flowers should be trimmed away as these will count against you.

Stage of growth. Sometimes flowers can only be bought in the same stage of growth. This is not always desirable as different sizes are attractive in a design. If you have a bunch of roses all in bud, then you can encourage some to open by placing them in a warm room. Others can be kept in a very cold place – perhaps the refrigerator – to stop them from opening, while a third group may

139

Above: An expressive abstract design called 'Stems'. Ivy is used to show strength, dried and sliced giant hogweed stems suggest cellular structure, the crosscut of walnut implies maturity, the container is like a tree trunk
Opposite: This garlanded figurine makes a lovely exhibition piece for a flower festival. Freesias, anemones, carnations, chrysanthemums and variegated foliage have been used to make the garland

be left in a cool place, so that they only open a little. In this way the roses will be at varying stages of maturity for the show.

Remember that the room in which the show is held may be very warm, especially in the summer, although the show committee will do their best to keep it cool. You must, therefore, make allowance for this and it is wise not to take very mature flowers to the show as they will soon become overblown. Choosing flowers at just the right stage of maturity is one of the things one learns with practice.

Transportation

Pack everything that you can the day before the show to avoid a rush, using your list to check that you have included everything. You will need:

Mechanics	Wire
Container	Watering-can
Plant Material	The show's schedule
Base*	Thermos of coffee*
Accessories*	Sandwiches*
Drape*	Spray can of water
Background*	Damp cloth
Flower scissors	Small towel
A sheet of polythene	

*if desired

Containers, bases, accessories. These can be wrapped in newspaper or sheets of soft plastic foam (not the kind used for supporting plant material) which can be bought at multiple stores and markets, and is excellent for preventing breakages. Pack them carefully in a large cardboard box, or a shopping basket, placing the heavy things at the bottom.

Drape. A creased drape can so easily lose you a prize and this is a pity as often it is not a necessary component. It is wise to press it well and roll it carefully on a cardboard roller. Then wrap it in paper to protect it from dirt. Many people are now using boards for backing their designs instead of drapes. The colours and textures of these can give wonderful atmosphere. There are various ways of making them. They can be covered with paint; Fablon; hessian with an adhesive backing; fabrics of all kinds; plaster of Paris; wallpaper; cork sheets; plastics; wood veneer.

Plant material. After conditioning foliage it should be packed in polythene bags. It is helpful to use separate bags for each arrangement. Grey foliage can become too wet and lose its greyness if kept in a bag for a long time.

Flowers can be taken in a bucket of water. Buckets standing on the floor of a car can fall over but if half-filled with water and wedged with other objects it is possible to carry them successfully without any spillage. It is useful to have the bucket of water containing the flowers at the show, as it saves unpacking flowers from a box and finding water as soon as you get there.

Flowers may be packed in boxes instead of buckets and the florist can normally spare one. Plastic sheeting is undesirable for packing in warm weather as the flowers open too quickly, and holes in the box give better air circulation. Tissue paper can be placed, crumpled, under each flower head to prevent damage.

It is wise to take a few spare flowers but a lot of extra plant material 'that you might want' can be a nuisance and cause confusion. It is better to make decisions before going to the show and to take only a few extra flowers in case of damage in travelling.

Staging

It is convenient to find the spaces for your exhibits before carrying in everything. The spaces are normally allocated by the show committee, and are usually in alphabetical order. A card with your name on it will be placed on your space.

Work tables are often available on which to place your belongings. If not, try to keep near to your space so that everyone has a fair share of the available working room. It is wise to cover the table space you have been allocated with a sheet of clean polythene before beginning the arrangement, as the covering materials can easily become dirty and this spoils the look of your exhibit. Sometimes show committees use materials for covering tables which are wipeable but this is not always so.

It is wise *not* to look at other exhibits until you have almost finished your own as it can be rather unnerving. You really need to wear blinkers at first. However, if you have practised your arrangement at home you will have more confidence. Do not be concerned that your arrangement looks different from the others – it may be that very difference that the judge appreciates. After your arrangement is completed it is fascinating to see how others have interpreted the same class title and you can learn so much from their exhibits. It is not advisable to change your own at this stage.

Always make sure your mechanics are especially firm in show work as it is embarrassing if anything falls over. Firm mechanics are another thing to practise when having a mock-up beforehand.

After completing the arrangement, and before leaving the show, you may like to spray the plant material with a fine mist of water, which helps to keep it fresh. Be careful not to wet draperies or to overfill the container so that it leaks on to the table and looks unsightly.

After Judging

Examine the prizewinners carefully to see the reasons for their awards. This can be very helpful. Also read all the comments made on the entry cards and, if possible, talk to the judge who will be very helpful. Try not to be too disappointed if you do not win a prize as this takes practice and one learns so much from showing whether or not a prize is won.

The Judge

The judge is normally trained for the job of assessing flower arrangements and awarding prizes. It is useful to know why prizes are given to certain arrangements and not to others and the headings used by a judge when studying the exhibits. In some countries these headings are printed in the show schedule and the number of marks for each heading is shown. This number can vary according to the class. For example, if the show committee wishes a class to concentrate on beautiful colouring, 'colour' will be made a heading and will receive a large number of the marks awarded, usually out of a hundred. Again, interpretation of a theme may be the committee's choice of emphasis and this will then have more marks than anything else. Different countries use slightly different systems as a basis for judging. Judges also vary in their headings and in the emphasis given to each heading. However, it is safe to assume that the following headings are used by all judges to some extent.

Criteria for Judging Flower Arrangements

Conformance to the show schedule. If the exhibit does not conform to the show schedule, it is eliminated from the competition and the following headings are not regarded.
Schedule interpretation.
Condition of plant material.
Design.
Staging and grooming.
Distinction.

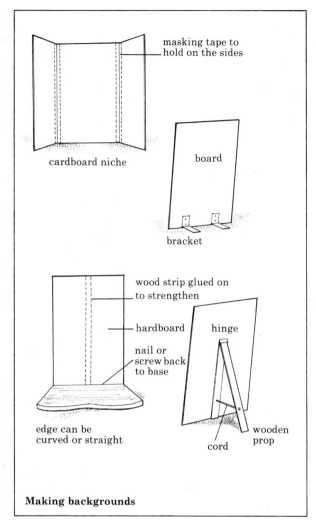

Making backgrounds

Conformance to the schedule. An exhibitor who has not followed the schedule will not be considered for a prize although the design may be excellent. A judge or a committee eliminates all those who have not followed the schedule before judging and these arrangements are normally left 'on exhibition only'. Study the wording over and over again, read any applicable handbook of schedule definitions and ask questions, if you have any doubts, to avoid disqualification.

Schedule interpretation. An exhibit may comply with the schedule but not interpret it very well. For example, in a class called 'Autumn Abundance', the exhibitor may have complied with the schedule requirements but presented a sparse design and not given the feeling of abundance. In a class called 'Daintiness, using plant material in tints', tints may have been used in the colouring but with rather larger flowers than the word daintiness suggests. Although complying with the schedule, the interpretations of the titles are not appropriate. Often you will see on an exhibit the judge's remark 'Good interpreta-

A design interpreting the 'Costa del Sol' and using a fisherman's wine carrier with geraniums, skeletonised prickly pear, driftwood and shells from that coast

tion of the schedule', or 'Well suited to this class', meaning that the exhibit not only complies with the wording of the schedule but also interprets the title, giving a suitable atmosphere.

Condition. The plant material must be in good condition and not wilting. Prizes are rarely given to an exhibit, however beautiful, if the plant material is not fresh, with turgid stems.

Design. The judge will assess the arrangement for good design. Although it is important to interpret the schedule well the exhibit should also be based on the good use of the principles of design. Judges vary on whether the interpretation of the

schedule or the design is the more important but most judges tend to make interpretation of the schedule the more important criterion, as there is no point in having a schedule if exhibitors do not try to interpret it.

Staging and grooming. The judge will look to see if the exhibit is well groomed. The plant material should have all damaged leaves and flowers trimmed away and should be clean and healthy.

Containers should be clean, drapes well pressed, bases neat. Good workmanship is essential and wires and other mechanics should not be visible.

A judge's remark often seen is 'Good staging'.

Distinction. A design which is distinctive may have several other attributes. In addition to following and interpreting the schedule well, having plant material in good condition, being well designed, groomed and staged, the following are normally appreciated:

ORIGINALITY. This means the exhibitor will have tried to be creative and to do something different, such as arranging unusual plant material; assembling a new style of design; using a container which shows good use of unexpected resources; including an original background or accessory. Originality should, however, be used in conjunction with the use of good design principles.

DISCRIMINATION. A careful choice of components so that they harmonise beautifully and are in good taste.

RESTRAINT. A selective use of materials so that nothing unnecessary is placed in the design. Simple things are usually the most effective.

INSPIRATION. Sometimes this comes easily and at other times inspiration seems lacking. It is helpful to develop a 'seeing eye' as there is so much in our environment to give inspiration for flower arrangement.

EXPRESSION. The design should say something – beautiful colouring, lovely lines or moving atmosphere – and the exhibitor should have tried to bring out a quality in the materials or a combination of qualities for others to notice.

INTERPRETATIVE ARRANGEMENTS

Many classes in shows ask for an exhibit which interprets subject matter, and this is rather different from a purely decorative design. The most important consideration is the message conveyed by the exhibit and *not* its decorative qualities. For example, 'A Pedestal Arrangement' asks only for a lovely flower arrangement on a pedestal but a class called 'Interpreting Winter' asks for an arrangement which really 'speaks' winter, in cold colours with little fresh plant material, and the result is unlikely to be decorative. The judge will look for the best interpretation of winter and not the most decorative or 'easy to live with' arrangement. Any style may be used for interpretative designs, accepted or original, and beauty in the sense of prettiness is not a criterion of their quality.

Interpretative designs are a recent interest. Symbolism, on the other hand, has been used for centuries; the Egyptians considered the lotus a symbolic flower; the madonna lily was sacred in Renaissance times; many flowers were symbolic to the Chinese, the narcissus meaning good wishes for the New Year and the orchid representing fertility; the Victorians sent messages through flowers as each flower had a meaning. However, interpretative flower arrangements which, through plant material, show the meaning of a given subject, express a mood, tell a story, make an observation on life or create an atmosphere, are of the present day. They are very fascinating. It is most interesting at a competitive flower arrangement show to see how several competitors interpret the same subject. They tend to look quite different because of each flower arranger's background, experiences and feelings. The prizewinners are normally those whom the judge considers interpret the subject in the best way and with clarity.

One of the advantages of entering a class which asks for the interpretation of a subject is that it leads the exhibitor into other fields. You may be asked to interpret 'The Gypsy Life' or 'In the Time of the Pharaohs', both of which would need some research in order to give the appropriate atmosphere. Many subjects may be chosen by the show committee. The theme may be the title of a book, play, film, piece of music. It may ask for an interpretation of a scene, such as 'The Mountainside', or of a season, such as 'High Summer'. It may ask for an event such as 'May Day', an atmosphere such as 'Richness' or a mood such as 'Gaiety'. It is good practice to make arrangements at home and then think of a title for them or ask the family to suggest a name.

How to Create an Interpretative Design

1. Write down words associated with the subject matter using the headings listed on page 138.
2. Use as few materials as possible to suggest the subject. Understatement is usually more effective than overstatement and the viewer's imagination will fill in the rest of the picture. When interpreting 'Holiday by the Sea' it is unnecessary to include a bucket, a spade, shells, sand, a beach ball and sunglasses. Each one of those is suggestive of a beach but if all are used then the plant material becomes overwhelmed with accessories. When interpreting another country use an authentic accessory if possible and not one sold only to tourists. Often the message can be conveyed by the plant material without the use of accessories.
3. Make sure that every component in the design helps to interpret the subject. For example, if the class is 'The British Countryside' then wild

flowers, a stone base and moss are quite suitable, but a Chinese antique base would be most unsuitable and would destroy the atmosphere of unsophistication.

4. Try to gain first-hand experience of the subject to be interpreted. If this is not possible, then look through books or talk to knowledgeable people about it. A visit to a lakeside will reveal many little things which you had forgotten – the type of plant material, the way it leans in one direction, stones peeping out of the water, a bird's feather nearby and so on.

5. Do not be afraid of omitting flowers if they do not seem suited to the subject. A class called 'Wintertime, a landscape design' may be better interpreted with bare branches, a stone base and a few evergreen leaves than with white carnations. These may suggest the colour and coldness of winter but would not be suitable plant material because they would not be seen growing out of doors in mid-winter.

6. Plant materials can be used to suggest a subject through their association; wild flowers are associated with the countryside and naturalness; plants grown in a greenhouse may be associated with luxury, richness, sophistication; upright growing plant materials such as sansevieria and iris may suggest dignity, aspiration; curved plant material such as willow, ivy, aspidistra may suggest grace; thorny plant material may be used for cruelty; bare branches for frugality; fruit for abundance; driftwood for strength. It is an interesting exercise to look at a piece of plant material and then to think of an abstract word to go with it.

7. Containers may help the interpretation through their shape, colour, texture, and the materials of which they are made. Glass and silver are usually elegant; stoneware is rugged and less sophisticated; basketry is informal and so on.

8. The manner of assembling the design can contribute to the interpretation: a narrow vertical design suggests dignity, elegance, austerity; an overflowing design suggests abundance; a sparse one may be frugality; a diagonal design may suggest speed; a horizontal one stillness or repose.

9. Colours can be a very great help in interpretation and there are many associations, although these can vary from country to country and civilisation to civilisation. Often it is not the hue but the modification of the hue which is the most expressive. For example, a tint of violet may suggest gentle modesty but a dark shade of violet may suggest mystery.

When you have some spare time or can persuade the family to join in a 'party game', it is a good idea to list the hues and neutrals together with the associations that they bring to mind. For example, red will represent anger, fire, courage and so on, while green implies rest, coolness and jealousy. There are many more.

Practical Arrangements

Create designs which interpret the following:

Another country	The seashore
A mood	Green pastures
Springtime	Tranquillity
Spring song	Anger
Frugality	Harvest
Daintiness	Youth and age
A book title	Thanksgiving
In grandmother's day	Purity
Storm	Ambition
Rhapsody in blue	Drama

THE USE OF ACCESSORIES

If a show schedule states that a handbook of schedule definitions will be used as a basis for judging, then the word 'accessory', with its definition, can usually be found in it. The definition normally includes objects such as bottles, figurines, plates, candles, boxes, which are made of substance other than plant material or, if made of wood (which is plant material), have been carved or moulded so that there is no longer a natural appearance.

Sometimes an accessory such as a candle may be placed *in* the container with the flowers. At other times an accessory may be placed at the side or in the middle of the flowers. It may or may not touch the plant material. It may be used in interpretative classes at a flower arrangement show to suggest the subject and stir the imagination. It can also be used in a decorative design to add beauty and to stretch the flowers when they are scarce, such as during winter in Britain. Using accessories with flowers is not new and the first were used in the time of the Egyptians who incorporated metal animals into their containers, which could be seen through the flowers.

How to Include an Accessory

1. Place it in position before adding any plant material whenever possible. It should take the place of plant material which would be needed if the accessory were not used and the design should seem lacking in something if the accessory is taken away when the arrangement is complete.

The total design of container, base, plant material *and* accessory should give a unified and complete effect.

2. A base, on which both flower arrangement and accessory stand, is helpful as it draws the two together and the accessory seems more a part of the design.

3. When more than one accessory is used in a design, they look better grouped and not scattered haphazardly about. Their composition is important and various positions should be tried.

4. When an accessory is used to help the interpretation of a subject, it should either be entirely suitable or it should be omitted. The use of accessories is not a necessity to interpretative work and it is better to let the flowers interpret the subject than to use an accessory in poor taste or one which is not suited to the subject.

5. Natural material, such as stones, feathers, shells, coral, is the easiest to use with plant material. Objects of real beauty, such as glass bottles, carved figurines and porcelain, are also easy to use.

6. The accessory should harmonise with the plant material, base and container.

Size. The accessory should be in scale with the other components. It is not attractive to have the flower arrangement and the accessory of equal size and since the present generation feels that the plant material should be the most important, then the accessory should be smaller. However, it should not appear dwarfed by the flowers. If an accessory does seem too small it can be drawn to the front of the design to make it appear bigger, and an accessory which seems too big should be placed to the back of the arrangement. Placing some of the plant material across the accessory also reduces its size and impact. Sometimes an accessory can look more important when it is lifted up amongst the flowers on a small stand, which may or may not be hidden by plant material.

Colour. The accessory seems more a part of the design if one or more of its colours are repeated in the plant material.

Shape. The shape of the accessory can be repeated in the plant material. For example, flowers can be curved around a plate to follow its curved lines or a tall figurine may be placed next to a vertical flower arrangement.

Texture. The texture of the accessory may provide a necessary contrast to the textures of the other components.

Style. An accessory which is traditional in appearance, such as a figurine of metal, should be accompanied by a traditionally styled flower

'Simply Dignity' a vertical arrangement to harmonise with the figure

arrangement. A modern semi-abstract figurine needs a more modern flower arrangement.

Practical Arrangements using Accessories

(A) A water arrangement incorporating stones.
(B) A design which includes a plate on a stand.
(C) A design which includes a figurine.
(D) A design which incorporates a glass bottle.
(E) A design which complements a painting.
(F) An arrangement of flowers with a grouping of fruit beside it.
(G) An arrangement of flowers with a second and smaller flower arrangement placed beside it.

The shape of the accessory repeated in the design

A Flower Arranger's Collection

A good flower arranger needs a stock of materials to use in designs, including plant material, containers, bases, mechanics and accessories of all kinds. A selection is a necessity for flower arranging anywhere – homes, churches or flower arrangement shows. It takes some time to build up such a stock but this is something that should not be hurried and only the most useful and beautiful things added. Collecting is also part of the fun of being a flower arranger and many happy hours can be spent searching for suitable plants and objects. There is great delight in finding something unexpected on a country walk, in woodland, by lake and seashore. Antique shops, auction sales, markets and craft studios are continually fascinating providing containers and accessories of all descriptions. Nurseries and garden centres are happy hunting grounds for interesting plants. The whole of our environment is full of many treasures for the flower arranger and one only needs to develop a seeing eye to discover them.

An essential part of any collection is a group of useful plants from which to cut flowers, branches and foliage. It is sensible to plant a basic collection in the garden as soon as you become interested in flower arrangement because some plants take a while to become fully established. People without gardens can plant a surprising amount of useful material in window boxes and pots in the house.

The problem is what to select from the vast number of plants available. It is wise to start with material that is easy to grow and if possible has a double use: foliage that is useful for cutting and also for preserving with glycerine; flowers that can be used both fresh and dried; plants that provide all-the-year-round foliage. As you learn more about flower arrangement and see interesting plant material at flower club demonstrations and flower arrangement shows, in gardens, in newspapers and magazines, then this may be added to the basic collection.

Flowers can be bought all the year round from flower shops and there is never a real shortage, but foliage is another matter – it may sometimes be bought but supplies are limited and there is little variation. So if the garden is small it is wise to concentrate on plants which provide good foliage for cutting.

A SELECTION OF PLANT MATERIAL TO GROW

The following are basic collections which are easy to grow and hardy in most parts of the British Isles. They are outdoor plants unless otherwise stated. A good book on gardening will help with their cultivation.

KEY TO ABBREVIATIONS USED IN THE LISTS
A: annual or biennial
B: bulb, corms, tubers
C: climber or wall plant
E: evergreen
P: perennial
S: shrub
T: tree
Pr: preserves with glycerine

Fifteen Useful Plants for Beginners

These have been selected by a group of flower arrangement teachers.

Alchemilla mollis (Lady's Mantle). P. Small round leaves and small yellow flowers in summer.

Aucuba japonica longifolia (Laurel). E S. Lanceolate bright green leaves all year. Pr.

Bergenia cordifolia. P. Large round leaves colouring in autumn, pink flowers in spring. Pr.

Corylus avellana contorta (Hazel, Harry Lauder's Walking Stick). S. Very curved branches for winter use.

Cytisus praecox (Broom). S. Early flowers and foliage for lines.

Elaeagnus pungens variegata. E S. Yellow-edged green foliage all the year. Pr.

Escallonia Apple Blossom. E S. Pink flowers in summer, branches for lines.

Hedera canariensis variegata (Ivy). E C. Silvery-grey and green foliage all year for curving lines. Any variegated ivy is useful. Pr.

Hosta sieboldiana, or any hosta (Plantain Lily). P. Useful oval leaves of varied colours and markings. Pr.

Iris pallida. B. Long straight leaves.

Ligustrum ovalifolium aureum (Golden Privet). E S. Yellow and green leaves for lines and transitional shapes.

Lonicera japonica aureoreticulata (Japanese Honeysuckle). E C. Curved yellow and green foliage for lines.

Lunaria annua (Honesty). A. Flowers, leaves and seed heads useful.

Mahonia Charity. E S. Graceful foliage for lines and transitional shapes, deep yellow flowers in autumn and winter. Pr.

Sedum spectabile. P. Long season for flowers and foliage.

Foliage for Use All the Year

Aucuba japonica longifolia (Laurel). E S. Green leaves, generally useful. Pr.

Bergenia cordifolia purpurea (round leaves) and *Bergenia crassifolia* (ovate leaves). P. Good for covering mechanics. Pr.

Buxus sempervirens latifolia maculata (Box). E S. Small green leaves blotched with yellow. Pr.

Calluna vulgaris H. E. Beale (Heather). E S. Also the double pink flowers dry well.

Camellia japonica. E S. Glossy green leaves also lovely flowers. Pr.

Chamaecyparis obtusa crippsii (Cypress). E T. Golden foliage in fern-like sprays.

Choisya ternata (Mexican Orange Blossom). E S. Needs a sheltered position, shining dark green leaves. Pr.

Cytisus praecox (Broom). S. Good curves of arching green stems. Pr.

Elaeagnus pungens variegata. E S. Green leaves with creamy-yellow margins. Pr.

Elaeagnus macrophylla. E S. Grey-green foliage. Pr.

Escallonia Apple Blossom, pink flowers, or Glory of Donard, red flowers. E S. Good curving branches.

Euonymus fortunei Silver Queen. E C. Green leaves with creamy-white margins. Pr.

Fatsia japonica (*Aralia sieboldii*). E S. Large polished dark green leaves. Pr.

Hedera canariensis variegata (Ivy). E C. Silvery grey and green leaves. Pr.

Hedera colchica dentata variegata (Ivy). E C. Yellow and green leaves. Pr.

Hedera helix Buttercup (Ivy). E C. Yellow foliage.

Hosta crispula, one of many useful species of hosta

Helleborus corsicus, *H. foetidus.* E P. Pr.

Ilex aquifolium Bacciflava (Holly). E S. Yellow berries, green leaves, Pr.

Ilex aquifolium Golden Queen (Holly). E S. Gold and green leaves. Pr.

Ligustrum ovalifolium aureum (Golden Privet). E S. Golden and green foliage.

Lonicera japonica aureoreticulata (Japanese Honeysuckle). E C. Good curving trails of yellow and green foliage.

Mahonia Charity. E S. Long spiny leaflets. Pr.

Pittosporum crassifolium. E S. Needs wall protection, thick dark green leaves, white felted underneath. Pr.

Polystichum (hardy ferns). E.

Salvia officinalis Icterina (Sage). Semi-E S. Green and gold leaves.

Skimmia japonica. E S. Green leathery leaves, also good berries on female plants. Pr.

Thuja plicata aureovariegata. E S. Yellow and green fern-like foliage.

Viburnum rhytidophyllum. E S. Large oval green leaves. Pr.

Viburnum tinus (Laurustinus). E S. Glossy dark green leaves. Pr.

Vinca major elegantissima (Periwinkle). E S. Variegated white and green trailing foliage.

Line Plant Material

Berberis thunbergii atropurpurea (Barberry). S. Dark red foliage.

Macleaya cordata has handsome, sculptured foliage

Corylus avellana contorta (Hazel, Harry Lauder's Walking Stick). S. Very curved winter branches.
Curtonus paniculatus. B. Long slender leaves which press well.
Cytisus praecox (Broom). S. Good curves of arching stems, creamy flowers in spring. Pr.
Elaeagnus pungens variegata. E S. Yellow-edged green foliage. Pr.
Elaeagnus macrophylla. E S. Grey-green foliage. Pr.
Escallonia Apple Blossom. E S. Pink flowers in summer and evergreen foliage.
Gladiolus. B. Tall narrow leaves.
Iris pallida dalmatica. B. Tall narrow leaves, also *argentea* (silver stripes) *aurea* (gold stripes).
Ligustrum ovalifolium aureum (Golden Privet). E S. Yellow and green leaves.
Lonicera japonica aureoreticulata (Japanese Honeysuckle). E C. Good trails of yellow and green foliage.
Lonicera tellmanniana (Honeysuckle). C. Yellow flowers in summer and good trails.
Macleaya cordata (Plume Poppy). P. Tall brown flowers in summer, useful leaves.
Phormium tenax (New Zealand Flax). E P. Green, *atropurpureum*, purple and *variegatum* yellow green and white. All have very tall narrow leaves and need a sheltered position.
Polygonatum (Solomon's Seal). P. Green leaves with curved stems. Pr.

Prunus Fudanzakura (Japanese Cherry). T. Flowering branches.
Salix matsudana tortuosa (Willow). T. Curved winter branches.
Salix setsuka (Willow). S. Fasciated winter branches.
Sorbus aria lutescens (Whitebeam). T. Almost white early foliage on branches. Pr.
Spiraea bumalda Anthony Waterer. S. Flowering branches of crimson flowers in summer.
Weigela florida variegata. S. Flowering branches – pink flowers in summer, cream-edged leaves.

Grey Foliage

Cineraria maritima Diamond. P. White leaves. A half-hardy plant which can be raised from seed each year.
Onopordum acanthium (Scotch Thistle). P. Big grey leaves.
Rosa rubrifolia. S. Blue-grey rose foliage.
Ruta graveolens. E S. Blue-grey small leaves.

Useful Deciduous Foliage

Acer pseudoplatanus brilliantissimum. T. Apricot-coloured spring foliage.
Arum italicum pictum. P. Useful winter foliage.
Hosta crispula (white margin to the dark green leaves), *H. fortunei* Albopicta (pale green edge to yellow leaves), *H. fortunei aureo-marginata* (pale gold margin), *H. sieboldiana* (silvery-grey leaves), *H. elata* (large dark green leaves), *H. undulata* (wavy leaves with white markings).
Lunaria annua (Honesty). A. May remain on the plant all winter.
Pelargonium (Geranium). P.
Sempervivum tectorum Commander Hay (Common Houseleek). Succulent, hardy enough to survive out of doors all year. Useful for points.

Berries, Hips and Catkins

Cotoneaster Cornubia. Semi-E S. Red berries in autumn.
Garrya elliptica. E S. Green-grey catkins in late winter.
Hypericum calycinum (Rose of Sharon). S. Black fruits in autumn.
Ilex aquifolium Bacciflava (Holly). E S. Yellow berries in autumn and winter.
Phytolacca americana (American Pokeberry). P. Black berries (poisonous) in autumn.
Pyracantha atalantioides. E S. Red berries in autumn and winter.

Rosa moyesii. S. Bottle-shaped red hips in autumn.

Salix wehrhahnii (Willow). S. Silvery-grey catkins in spring.

Skimmia japonica. E S. Red berries in late summer and autumn, but only on female plants. *S. foremanii* produces berries on all plants.

Symphoricarpos albus laevigatus (Snowberry). S. White berries in autumn and winter.

Viburnum opulus. S. Red fruits in autumn and winter.

Flowers for Drying by the Hanging Method

Achillea Coronation Gold (Yarrow). P. Deep yellow flowers in summer.

Achillea Moonshine (Yarrow). P. Pale yellow flowers in summer.

Allium aflatunense, *A. giganteum, A. cepa* (Onion), *A. porrum* (Leek), *A. moly, A. albopilosum.* B. Rounded flower heads in white, yellow, purple or blue produced in spring and summer.

Anaphalis margaritacea (Pearly Everlasting). P. Small white flowers in summer.

Astilbe. P. Plume-like heads of small flowers in red, pink and white in summer.

Astrantia major (Hattie's Pincushion). P. Small flowers, white or pink, in summer.

Calluna vulgaris H. E. Beale (Heather). E S. Bright pink double flowers in late summer and autumn.

Cynara scolymus (Globe Artichoke). P. Round or conical heads with purple thistle-like flowers in late summer and autumn, also good leaves.

Cynara cardunculus (Cardoon). P. Similar to the globe artichoke but smaller and with spine-tipped flowers in late summer.

Delphinium. P. Blue, white or pink spurred flowers in summer.

Delphinium consolida (Larkspur). A. Red, pink, mauve or white spurred flowers in summer.

Echinops ritro (Globe Thistle). P. Blue rounded flowers in summer. Pick flowers before they come out.

Eryngium alpinum, *E. giganteum, E. variifolium* (Sea Holly). P. Blue, grey and green flowers in summer.

Helichrysum bracteatum Dwarf Spangle Mixed or Double Mixed (Straw Flower). A. Mixed colours, daisy-type flowers in summer.

Helipterum roseum. A. Mixed colours, daisy-like flowers.

Hydrangea, Hortensia varieties. S. All colours from pink to purple and blue. Also *H. cinerea sterilis,* S. Small white flowers.

Limonium sinuatum New Art Shades (Sea

The very decorative seed heads of *Iris foetidissima*

Lavender, Statice). A. Flowers in a mixture of pastel colours produced in summer.

Grasses for Drying

Briza maxima (Quaking Grass). A.

Bromus (Ornamental Oats). A.

Cortaderia (Pampas Grass). E P.

Lagurus ovatus (Hare's Tail Grass). A.

Miscanthus sinensis variegatus (Giant Grass, Eulalia). P.

Triticum (Ornamental Wheat). A.

Seed Heads for Drying

Alliums as listed under flowers for drying by the hanging method.

Angelica archangelica. P.

Ballota pseudodictamnus. P.

Centaurea dealbata. P.

Crocosmia masonorum. B.

Delphinium, Belladonna hybrids. P.

Digitalis (Foxglove). A and P. Glycerining seed heads is even better than drying.

Dipsacus follonum (Teasel). A.

Iris foetidissima. B.

Lunaria annua (Honesty). A.

Nicandra physaloides (Shoo-fly Plant). A.

Nigella damascena (Love-in-a-mist). A.

Papaver somniferum, Paeony-flowered Mixed (Peony Poppy). A. *P. rhoeas* (Corn or Shirley

Astrantia major has unusual and pretty flowers

Poppy), double forms. A.
Papaver orientale (Oriental Poppy). P.
Physalis franchetii (Chinese Lantern). P.
Verbascum bombyciferum. A.

Useful Flowers

Normally these cannot be bought at florists.
Alchemilla mollis (Lady's Mantle). P. Long flowering small yellow flowers in summer.
Amaranthus (Love-lies-bleeding). A. Trailing red or green flowers in summer.
Anthemis tinctoria Mrs E. C. Buxton and *A. tinctoria* Grallagh Gold (Chamomile). P. Both with yellow daisy-like flowers in summer, excellent for pressing.
Astrantia major (Hattie's Pincushion). P. Small white or pink flowers produced in summer.
Ceanothus Autumnal Blue. E S. Autumn flowers.
Euphorbia polychroma and *E. palustris.* P. Bright yellow flowers, long early season.
Euphorbia griffithii Fireglow. P. Red flowers.
Hamamelis mollis (Witch Hazel). S. Yellow flowers in winter.
Helleborus. P. Winter and early spring flowers in white, pink and purple.
Heuchera. P. Flowers in shades of pink and red for most of the summer.
Hydrangea. S. Many varieties varying in colour from pink and purple to blue.
Jasminum nudiflorum (Winter Jasmine). S. Yellow flowers in winter.
Kniphofia (Red-hot Poker). P. Spikes of flowers in late summer and autumn. Colours in variations of red, orange and yellow.
Lilium. B. (Some can be bought). Many kinds and varieties.
Nicotiana (Tobacco Plant). A. Long-flowering season, small flowers in green, crimson or white.
Prunus subhirtella autumnalis and *P. s. a. rosea.* T. Small winter flowers in white and pale pink respectively.
Rudbeckia bicolor superba. A. and *R. fulgida* Goldsturn and *R.f. speciosa* (Cone Flower). P. Yellow and chestnut-red flowers in summer.
Salvia horminum Monarch Bouquet (Clary). A. Bracts are very colourful and in mixed colours in this variety.
Tellima grandiflora. P. Erect flower spikes in green in late spring and summer.
Viburnum opulus sterile (Snowball Bush). S. Greenish-white round flowers in summer.
Viburnum bodnantense Dawn. S. Fragrant pink flowers in late autumn and winter.

Roses

Roses may be bought from the florist all the year round but the following are a few of those loved by flower arrangers which cannot usually be bought as cut flowers.

Old Roses

Alba:
Königin von Dänemark, pink
Bourbon:
Boule de Neige, white double rounded flowers
Mme Pierre Oger, blush pink
La Reine Victoria, deep pink
Mme Isaac Pereire, deep pink
Centifolia:
Petite de Holland, pale pink
Fantin Latour, warm pink
China:
Rose chinensis viridiflora, small green double flowers. A curiosity but useful.
Gallica:
Cardinal de Richelieu, pinkish purple
Charles de Mills, maroon
Hybrid Perpetual:
Reine des Violettes, purple-red
Empereur de Maroc, deep crimson
Roger Lambelin, unusual shape like a carnation, deep red streaked with white, needs good cultivation.
Souvenir du Docteur Jamain, red-purple
Moss:
Gloire des Mousseux, deep pink

Other Roses

Amberlight, floribunda, orange and brown
Artistic, floribunda, golden-brown
Blue Moon, hybrid tea, silvery lilac
Brownie, floribunda, deep pink/bronze
Constance Spry, modern shrub, pink, old shape
Fairy Dancers, floribunda, small, blush pink
Fantan, hybrid tea, orange/yellow
Grey Pearl, hybrid tea, pale grey/pink
Handel, modern climber, cream/pink
Iceberg, floribunda, white
Jocelyn, floribunda, brown/purple
Lake Como, floribunda, lilac, wavy-edged petals
Lavender Lassie, modern shrub, lilac/pink
Magenta, floribunda shrub, deep lilac, old shape
News, floribunda, purple
Rosa cantabrigiensis, species, fern-like leaves which colour well in autumn.
Rosa rubrifolia, species, grey leaves.
Rosa moyesii Geranium, species, good hips
Rosemary Rose, floribunda, rosy red, prolific, old shape
Silver Charm, floribunda, mauve, single
The Wife of Bath, modern shrub, shell pink
Tom Brown, floribunda, two-tone brown
Vesper, floribunda, soft orange/brown
Whisky Mac, hybrid tea, gold/bronze

Useful Indoor Plants

Aspidistra. E. House plant. Pr.
Begonia rex. E. House plant. Foliage in striking colours and markings, grey, green, red.
Cissus antarctica. E. House plant. Serrated oval green leaves.
Cobaea scandens. C. Purple and green flowers.
Fatshedera lizei. E. House plant. Hardy out of doors in some districts. Pr.
Gardenia jasminoides. E S. White fragrant summer flowers.
Grevillea robusta. E S. Fast growing. Fern-like leaves. Pr.
Griselinia lucida. E S. Hardy in some districts. Pr.
Nephrolepis cordifolia. Fern. E.
Nephrolepis cordifolia plumosa. Fern. E.
Pteris ensiformis victoriae. Fern. E. Segments banded in white.
Pelargonium crispum variegatum. Sub-shrub. E. Fan-shaped, lobed leaves.
Ricinus (Castor-oil Plant). P.
  Aucuba, *Vinca rosea, Camellia japonica,* polystichum, hosta, *Lilium auratum, Lilium speciosum rubrum,* may also be grown indoors when a garden is not available and all are useful. Helichrysum,

Mme Pierre Oger, one of the lovely Bourbon roses

helipterum and *Nicotiana affinis* Lime Green may be grown in pots, as can many other annuals.

CONTAINERS

After plants, containers are the most important part of a flower arranger's collection, and there are very many to choose from. The use of water retaining plastic foam, and sometimes polythene to prevent leakage, has made it possible to use almost anything as a container. Descriptions of the many varieties available could fill several books.

In spite of containers being readily available, it is fun to make some at home and there is great pride in accomplishment. It is also possible to adapt certain existing objects to make attractive containers.

Adaptations

Electric lamp bases. These often have a tall, narrow neck for holding the electric light bulb. This is useful for flower arrangement as it lifts the plant material in an attractive manner, giving a lighter effect.

To adapt the lamp base: remove the electrical fitting, including the cord, with the exception of the cup-shaped piece of metal or plastic which fits into the lamp base. Glue a candlecup into this, using Araldite, Plastic Padding or any very strong glue.

Oil lamp bases. Old oil lamps make very attrac-

153

tive containers. Simply remove the glass funnel and the wick attachment and glue in a candlecup.

Metal figurines. There are many available with heavy bases which make them stable. Look for ones with a place on which to glue a small metal or plastic saucer. This may be on a lifted hand or a flat head. Glue the saucer on with Araldite, Plastic Padding or any strong glue. If no convenient flat place is available it is possible for a metal worker to fit a rod on to the base behind the figure and the saucer can be glued on to this.

Mechanics need to be light and the arrangement fairly small for this type of container, otherwise it may tip over.

Large round meat can. This makes an excellent base for various applied surfaces. Ask the butcher for any empty meat can of the type used for cooked meats. One end of the can should be left on and you may have to persuade him to do this for you. Cover the surface with one of the following:

(A) Bamboo canes split in half and glued on with Uhu or a similar contact glue.

(B) A metallised plastic tile, cut to fit and glued on.

(C) A straw mat, cut to fit and glued on.

(D) Plaster of Paris or Snowcem roughly applied, painted when dry and varnished with matt polyurethane.

(E) String wound around the can and glued on.

(F) Self-adhesive fabric or paper (e.g. Fablon) and there are many to choose from. Cut a strip with a $\frac{3}{4}$-in. margin top and bottom for folding over each end. To make a neat turn, clip the turning for almost $\frac{3}{4}$ in. in several places. Braid may be glued on to the edges.

(G) Add sand or grit to paint and cover the can with this. When dry it will have an interesting texture.

(H) Glue pebbles or seeds on to the surface. Paint over these for more permanency.

As the can is quite light it is easily tipped over. The best mechanics are, therefore, sand, which adds weight, with a pinholder placed on the top.

Bottle. An existing bottle of plain glass can be coloured by swilling paint around the inside until it is completely covered.

Containers to Make

From sheet lead. This can be bought from a plumber. It can be cut with strong scissors and moulded easily. It can also be re-shaped and it holds water. A shallow container can easily be made.

COMPONENTS

(A) Sheet of lead.

(B) Small wooden mallet.

(C) Block of rough wood about 2 in. by 3 in. by 3 in.

(D) Paper.

(E) Scissors.

(F) File.

(G) Ball-point pen.

(H) Heavy gloves (to prevent cut fingers).

METHOD

Cut a paper pattern of the intended base of the container, an asymmetrical shape is interesting. Draw around the pattern on the lead with the pen. Cut out the container, leaving a minimum of a $1\frac{1}{2}$-in. margin outside the marks (this will be the sides of the container). Turn up the sides by hammering them up with the mallet against the block of wood. File any sharp edges. Erase marks with steel wool.

A plaster of Paris container. A four-sided container, which is modern in appearance and may have many different surface textures, can be made with plaster of Paris.

COMPONENTS

(A) Plasticine. 3 lb. – makes two moulds for the larger sides.

(B) Water.

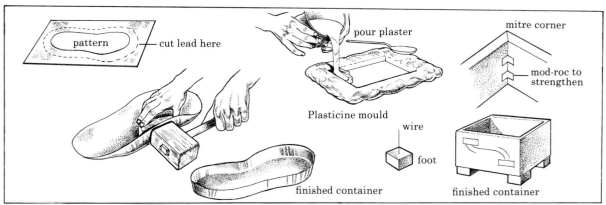

A container made from sheet lead and a plaster of Paris container

154

(c) Mixing bowl and spoon.
(d) File.
(e) Plaster of Paris in powder form. 3·175 kilo (7 lb.) bag.
(f) Knife.
(g) Small saw.
(h) Mod-roc (fabric re-inforced plaster for modelling).

METHOD

1. Make the mould. Warm the Plasticine and roll it into a flat block about 8 in. by 3½ in. and ½ in. deep, using a rolling pin. Make sure the sides are straight and even – they can be cut with a knife. This is the bottom of the mould. Add walls of Plasticine which rise about 1 in. higher than the bottom. Smooth the joins together so that there are no cracks between them.

2. Make the plaster. Add the powder to water, and not the reverse. Fill a basin half full of cold water and sieve the plaster through the fingers in a fine stream, making sure it spreads over the bottom of the basin and that the powder is not in a heap on the bottom. When the basin is nearly full, pour off the residue water and a fairly thick paste will be left in the bowl. Stir this thoroughly.

3. Make the sides of the container. Pour and spoon the plaster into the Plasticine mould *quickly* and until it comes almost to the top of the wall (about ¾ in.) Leave for two hours to set, but wash the bowl out at once. Remove the Plasticine mould. Make a second side of this size. Then make the two remaining sides, 4½ in. by 3½ in. and ½ in. deep, to complete the four sides of the container, which will hold a 3-in. pinholder.

4. Adding the texture. This should be done *before* making the plaster. After rolling out the Plasticine base of the mould, press into it any interesting objects such as nails and coins. Heavy objects are the best. Remove the objects before pouring the plaster into the mould. The plaster should be made a little more liquid than for the smooth-sided container described previously. (This is so that it will run easily into the pattern made on the mould.) Leave to set for six hours, instead of two, before removing the sides of the container from the mould, as the textured surface may chip off easily unless it is really dry.

5. Joining the sides. Smooth the edges with sand-paper, a file or a rasp. Cut off the inside corners all along the edges which will be joined, using a light saw. Mitre the edges. (This means cutting away plaster so that the two sides join at an angle of 90 degrees.) Scratch the surface of these cut edges slightly with a knife point and dampen them. Press the sides together. Dip a length of

Dried leaves and anthuriums in a home-made container

Mod-roc plaster into water and push into the mitred corner down the whole length on the inside to strengthen the joint. When set, mix a small amount of plaster with water until creamy and with a knife press this on to the joint to strengthen and neaten it.

6. Casting the bottom of the container. Place a flattened piece of Plasticine on to a flat surface and press the container on to it. Turn up some Plasticine outside the container to prevent leakages. Pour about ¾ in. of plaster on to the Plasticine and leave to set. A better joint is given if small grooves are made at the bottom of each of the sides of the container so that the plaster filters in to them.

This method makes a chunky type of container and a rough texture seems more suitable for the surface than a smooth one. An alternative way of making this type of container is to make a framework of ½-in.-mesh wire netting. Cover this with layers of dampened Mod-roc and smooth plaster of Paris over the surface.

The container may have feet or a base attached.

MAKING THE FEET. Flatten a piece of Plasticine on to a flat surface. Make 4 holes in it the size of the required feet. Pour plaster into these holes

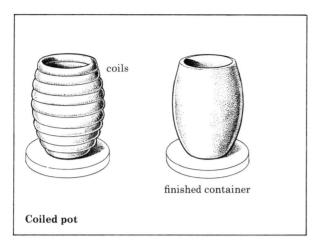

coils

finished container

Coiled pot

1. Model the base. This need not be coiled but can be cut to the size and shape you desire. Make a thick base because in order to remove the container from the turntable when it is complete, a piece of wire is used (like cutting cheese) and this takes away some of the base.

2. To make the coils, take a long piece of clay and roll it backwards and forwards on a board with the palm of the hand until it is about 2 ft. in length (longer is difficult to roll). The finished coil should be of even thickness and look like rope. Make several coils before beginning and wrap a damp cloth around them to keep them moist.

3. Make the pot by coiling the rolls of Plastone around and on top of each other. This may be done either continuously until each roll is finished, another one then being added, or each addition can be a separate ring broken from the roll. Smooth the sides in very firmly, after each addition, to make a compact pot. Leave to harden after removing from the turntable.

4. To colour the pot either add powder colour to the Plastone before making the pot, or make some Araldite into a solution with turpentine. Add powder paint to this and brush it on to the surface of the finished pot. This type of colouring dries very hard, rather like enamel, and it is very durable.

and push a length of heavy wire into them at once. Twist the wire for extra strength and leave ½ in. sticking out of the plaster, leave to set. Drill small holes in the bottom of the container where the feet are to be positioned. Dampen these and pour in a little plaster and then push the feet on at once so that the wire goes into the holes made in the bottom of the container. Leave to set.

COLOUR. This can be added to the container by various methods:
1. Add Kingston paint stains or wood stain to the water used for mixing the plaster.
2. Paint the completed container with any acrylic paint.
3. Add a few pinches of powder paint to the plaster at mixing time. Exciting results come from not mixing the paint in too well.
4. Leave flecks of powder paint on the bottom of the Plasticine mould.
5. Add wood stain to the surface when the container is finished.

WATERPROOFING: The container can be made waterproof by painting it with polyurethane varnish, which can be obtained with both matt and shiny surfaces. Apply more than one coat.

A coiled pot. Coiling is a pottery technique which does not require a potter's wheel. The pot is made out of lengths of rolled clay which are pressed together. Plastone is suitable for this work and does not need firing as it is self-hardening. It looks and feels like stone. If it is placed in an ordinary domestic oven to 'fire' it becomes even harder. Plastone tends to shrink when dry. There are other similar clays on the market.

COMPONENTS
(A) Self-hardening clay such as Plastone.
(B) A large board.
(C) A turntable.

DEVELOPING A SEEING EYE

Much of the joy of flower arranging lies in the discovery of the world around us and so many flower arrangers say, after being interested for a year or two, 'My eyes have been opened to a new world, and life can never be dull again'. Inspiration for design is everywhere, once you develop a seeing eye. At any time and in any place some object may await discovery and be the inspiration for a design. Your collection of plants, containers and accessories will suddenly begin to grow as you see design potential in all kinds of things in our environment.

In the Countryside

LOOK FOR AND COLLECT
Ferns for arranging and pressing.
Berries for autumn arrangements.
Grasses for drying.
Moss for covering pinholders and for retaining water.
Lichen and fungi to use in designs.
Bulrushes.
Branches with interesting shapes.

Driftwood.
Lichened branches for use in winter.
Stone in various colours for covering pinholders.
Tree stumps.
Bark for covering pinholders and using in plaques.
Leaves turning colour for pressing, especially in autumn.
Skeletonised leaves, under trees.
Willow catkins for drying.
Hazel catkins for spring arrangements.
Ivy trails for arrangements.
Ivy leaves for glycerining.
Ivy stems for line material.
Stone and slate for bases.
Toadstools for drying for landscape designs.
Birds nests (disused) for Flemish arrangements and landscapes.
Feathers.
Clean foliage for glycerining.
Pine cones.
Acorns.
Small wild flowers and leaves for pressing.
Iris seed pods by the lakesides.
Seed heads in the hedgerows.

It is wise to ask permission to pick things on private ground and to pick with restraint, remembering the importance of conservation of wild plant material.

STUDY
The colours of old brick walls, birds, the whites on a snowy day, dawn and sunset, autumn mists, butterflies' wings, mountains and water.
The sheen on the inside of a buttercup.
The daintiness of Queen Anne's Lace.
The formation of a spider's web.
Winter trees against the sky.
The way moss grows over stones.

The Seashore

LOOK FOR AND COLLECT
Feathers.
Grasses for drying.
Driftwood.
Stones of all colours.
Shells.
Seaweed to dry.
Coral, when abroad.
Pieces of old fishing net.
Flotsam and jetsam which have been attractively weathered.
Fishermen's floats of cork and glass.
Skates' eggs.
Bones.

Briza maxima, a grass to look for in the countryside

Limpets.
Loofah.
Sand for mechanics and drying.
Old rope.

STUDY
The colours in the landscape.
Stormy days for exciting colour schemes.
Rock pools for colour and shapes.
The angle at which grasses lean in the wind.
The plants which grow by the sea.

Stately Homes

COLLECT
Postcards of interiors and objects.

STUDY
Paintings for colour and composition.
Porcelain and beautiful containers for shape.
Settings and colour schemes.
The rooms, and imagine the flower arrangements you would place in them.
The landscaping of the garden and grounds.
The names of the plants in the garden.

Cities and Towns

LOOK FOR AND COLLECT
Containers, bases and accessories of all types from antique shops, market stalls, craft studios, potteries, department stores and china shops.
Remnants of all kinds of fabric for making bases and drapes.
Mats and antique stands for bases.
Old machinery for possibly adapting into containers.
Ask for scrap metal, rusty wire from technical school dumps.

157

Waste glass and plastic from factories.
Old discarded drainpipes for containers.
Old roof slate for bases.
Interesting candles in good colours.
Jugs, baskets, figurines, candlesticks, old teapots, pans, carved wooden boxes as well as the more usual containers.
Beautiful lace, tweed, silks, to combine with flowers.
New materials and interesting flowers and plants from flower shops.
Marble and stone bases from stonemasons.

STUDY
Museums to look at ancient objects and to gain atmosphere.
Art galleries to look at paintings and collect prints and postcards.
Exhibitions of sculpture, needlework and any other art or craft from which design can be learnt and techniques adapted.
Theatre design in sets and costumes.
Shop window display, especially at Christmas time.
Design centres for design in many objects.
Petals, crystals, wood graining under a microscope.
Bookshops for art, craft, gardening and flower arrangement books.
Libraries for poems and prose which inspire, books on crafts which are helpful such as pottery, tie-dyeing, basketry; also gardening and flower arrangement books.

Other Countries

COLLECT
Unusual plant material. If dried it can be brought into the United Kingdom without a licence. If fresh and rooted a licence should be obtained from the Department of Agriculture before travelling. This is not difficult. In other countries the correct procedure should be adhered to, otherwise you will lose your plants.
Containers and accessories, typical of the country.
Stones.
Shells and coral.
Driftwood.
Fabrics.

STUDY
The colours of the landscapes.
Costumes.
The type of plant material growing.
Museum, art galleries and exhibitions.
Historic places.

A FLOWER ARRANGER'S NOTEBOOK

Part of a good flower arranger's collection is her notebook. So many beautiful moments and experiences are soon forgotten and it can be difficult to recall them. Brief notes and sketches can stimulate the memory and bring so much back to mind. A notebook provides a record which is invaluable and this can be a private book – something in which you draw and write in your own special way. Many people do not find it easy to express themselves by drawing and yet it is one of the best ways of recording. It is not often used because lack of skill is embarrassing, but as this is your own notebook and not for publishing, then drawing talent is irrelevant. It is important to record objects, scenes, to make notes of colours, textures, and so on, for future inspiration.

Your notebook can also hold cuttings from newspapers and magazines to provide a storehouse of ideas.

Suggestions

A looseleaf book with lined and blank pages.
Grouping subject matter where possible for easy reference.

INCLUDE
Pictures of flower arrangements and plants from newspapers and magazines.
Photographs of your own arrangements and plants.
Articles about flower arrangement, plants and gardening.
Plant names collected at flower clubs and shows and by looking in nurseries, gardens and garden centres.
Drawings of the shapes of beautiful containers.
Notes on exciting colour schemes.
Drawings of landscape scenes, such as the side of a lake.
Lists of articles seen in one habitat and their colours.
Notes of the atmosphere of certain scenes or experiences, doing this for river and stream, sky, cliff, downs, seaside, roadside, cornfield, meadow. Note the flora, fauna and colours and other interesting features.
Drawings of flower arrangements, seen in various places.
Drawings of small things as a record, such as stones in a lake.
Anything to remind you of the lovely things which can inspire a flower arrangement.

Index

Abbreviations: b=black and white photograph or drawing
c=colour photograph